D0947221

TWAYNE'S WORLD AUTHORS SERIES
A Survey of the World's Literature

FRANCE

Maxwell A. Smith, Guerry Professor of French, Emeritus
The University of Chattanooga
Former Visiting Professor in Modern Languages
The Florida State University
EDITOR

Francis Ponge

TWAS 577

FRANCIS PONGE

By MARTIN SORRELL

University of Exeter

TWAYNE PUBLISHERS

A DIVISION OF G. K. HALL & CO., BOSTON

Copyright © 1981 by G. K. Hall & Co.

Published in 1981 by Twayne Publishers,
A Division of G. K. Hall & Co.
All Rights Reserved

Printed on permanent / durable acid-free paper and bound
in the United States of America

First Printing

Library of Congress Cataloging in Publication Data

Sorrell, Martin.
Francis Ponge.

(Twayne's world authors series; TWAS 577: France)
Bibliography: p. 149-52
Includes index.
1. Ponge, Francis.   2. Authors, French—20th
century—Bibliography.
PQ2631.0643Z815   841'.914   80-19178
ISBN 0-8057-6419-4

PQ
2631
O643Z815

For Marc and Anna

3/13/81 Pub. 10.36 2

472043

Contents

About the Author

Martin Sorrell took his B.A. at Oxford, and his M.A. at the University of Kent, with a thesis on French poetry between the World Wars. He is now Lecturer in French at the University of Exeter. In 1975-6, he was Visiting Assistant Professor at the College of William and Mary, Virginia.

He has published an annotated edition of Banville's *Rondels* (Exeter French Texts). His English translation, with introduction and notes, of Jacques Vaché's *Lettres de guerre*, has been published as part of the special Dada number of the *Journal of European Studies*. Besides this, Martin Sorrell has published articles on Alain-Fournier, Alphonse Allais, and Prévert.

Preface

Ponge first attracted major attention in 1942, with the publication of a volume entitled *Le Parti pris des choses*, composed of a series of texts of varying length whose dominant characteristic was their scrupulous analysis-cum-presentation of objects, the "choses" of the title. These texts, situated somewhere between the fable and the prose poem, have achieved a certain notoriety, for they are unlike any other twentieth-century French poetry. At first glance, Ponge's texts in *Le Parti pris des choses* seem to have done away altogether with the subjective voice; this is also true of his subsequent books of poems. There is no attempt, apparently, by the writer to establish his own viewpoint, nor indeed does there seem to be any regard or respect for the human presence in the world, except insofar as human beings can be reduced to the quality and status of objects. For the most part, Ponge has an equal disregard for the conventions of prosody. In short, he gives every indication of having broken with the codes of practice which had previously governed the subject matter, the treatment, and the form of French poetry.

Ponge has written much else besides poems of this controversial sort. He has never stopped pondering the aesthetic questions which his new approach has posed, and the result has been that there are as many books by Ponge about poetry as there are books of poems. Another curious and important feature of his work, which arises from his unflagging interest in the problems of how to write, is that on several occasions he merges theoretical and creative text, composing an entity of two constituents which, as it were, hold mirrors to each other. This kind of text shows as well as any Ponge's unswerving concern not merely with the material world of objects which surrounds him, but also with the writer's, and therefore by extension with every human being's, responsibility toward that world. The theme which perhaps runs most clearly through all of Ponge's creative writing, from *Douze petits écrits* of 1926 to *Nouveau Recueil* and *Le Savon* of 1967, is the wish to restore correct proportions to a world which mankind, including its poets, has unjustly and unwisely distorted in its lazy or arrogant neglect of it. A kind of mystic of the material world, Ponge wants us to look afresh at all that surrounds us, to respect and love it, so that there can be established the proper and harmonious relationship between the human and the nonhuman. Despite its first appearance, therefore, Ponge's work is about man as well as about things; not about man's emotional life, his daily activities, his successes and failures, but rather about man as one species among others, with limitations, responsibilities, and with one gift above all, that of language.

In the three-part division of this study, Ponge's theories about poetry will be examined in the first. This will involve a discussion of his hostility toward much of the poetry that has been written before him, as well as an examination of the bases of his own aesthetic. The second part will be devoted to Ponge's poetic method, both as a subject he has written about and as it is demonstrated in his poems. The final part will consist entirely of analyses of complete poems, chosen to illustrate as widely as possible Ponge's range and the questions dealt with in the first two parts. It is not the aim of this study to be comprehensive and exhaustive. For example, it is not possible in this format to go fully into the questions surrounding phenomenology, although some rudimentary discussion of it as it applies to Ponge's work will be supplied. If this branch of philosophy is not within my competence, neither are the linguistics and semiology of the *Tel Quel* group. As is pointed out in this study, the group has shown a certain interest in Ponge, and relevant details are given in the bibliography. Similarly, Ponge's relationship to the "nouveau roman," the French new novel, as commented on by Robbe-Grillet, will be touched upon briefly but not scrutinized.

Finally, Ponge's several books and essays on painting and the plastic arts will receive occasional mention and nothing more. This is not to deny their importance or interest. On the contrary, they make rewarding reading on the whole, especially as Ponge has tended to deal not only with well-established and famous figures, but also with several lesser-known contemporary artists. However, as this study is intended to be about Ponge as a man of literature, and in view of the limitations of space, there will be no examination of Ponge as art critic, except when something he has said about painting or sculpture illuminates an aspect of his literary work. He remains best-known as the poet committed to objects and to the material world, and it is the aim of this study to explore Ponge's

Preface

reasons for this commitment, to look at its implications for the practical business of writing, and to sample some of the end products, the poems themselves.

MARTIN SORRELL

University of Exeter.

Acknowledgments

Grateful acknowledgment is made to Éditions Gallimard for permission to quote from the work of Francis Ponge.

Chronology

1899 March 27, Francis Ponge born in Montpellier, where his father, Armand Ponge, is a bank manager. In the same year, the family moves to Nîmes.

1900 Family moves to Avignon, where they stay until 1909. Receives a private education, then attends the Lycée Frédéric-Mistral.

1909 Family moves to Caen. Attends Lycée Malherbe (until 1916).

1916- At Lycée Louis-le-Grand in Paris. In the preparatory class for
1917 the École Normale Supérieure ("Hypokhâgne").

1919 Joins Socialist party.

1921 *Esquisse d'une parabole*, a Socialist tract.

1923 On the production side with the Gallimard publishing house. Death of Armand Ponge. Leaves his job.

1926 *Douze petits écrits*. Suffers nervous exhaustion.

1930 Member of Breton's surrealist group.

1931 Marries Odette Chabanel. Takes job with the firm of Hachette.

1935 Birth of daughter Armande.

1936 Strike and sit-in at Hachette; becomes a union official.

1937 Joins Communist party. Discharged by Hachette. Unemployed.

1938 Insurance salesman, consultant, then underwriter for the Soleil-Aigle company.

1939 Mobilized.

1942 Regional editor at Bourg-en-Bresse for newspaper *Progrès de Lyon*. *Progrès* suppressed after German takeover of free zone. Takes part in Resistance movement in Southern France. *Le Parti pris des choses*.

1944 Literary editor of Communist weekly *Action*. Meets painters (Braque, Picasso, Fautrier, Dubuffet, etc.) and writes his first pieces about art. Sartre's essay "L'Homme et les choses" (on *Le Parti pris des choses*).

1948 *Proêmes. Le Peintre à l'étude*.

1950 *La Seine.*

1952 Teaches at Alliance Française in Paris until his retirement in 1964. Conversation with Reverdy and Breton broadcast on French radio. *La Rage de l'expression.*

1956 *NRF* "Hommage à Francis Ponge" number.

1957 Marriage of his daughter Armande.

1959 Receives the Légion d'honneur.

1961 Moves to Bar-sur-Loup, near Grasse, in Provence. *Le Grand Recueil.*

1965 *Pour un Malherbe. Tome premier.*

1966 Visiting professor at Columbia University until February 1967.

1967 *Le Savon. Nouveau Recueil.* Conversations between Ponge and Philippe Sollers broadcast on French radio.

1970 *Entretiens de Francis Ponge avec Philippe Sollers* (1967 conversations in book form).

1971 *La Fabrique du Pré.*

1973 Receives the Ingram Merrill Foundation International Prize for 1972.

1974 Receives the Books Abroad Neustadt International Literary Prize.

1975 Colloquium on "Ponge inventeur et classique" held in August at the Centre Culturel International, Cerisy-la-Salle.

1977 Proceedings of Cerisy colloquium published as *Francis Ponge: Colloque de Cerisy. Comment une figue de paroles et pourquoi. L'Atelier contemporain. L'Écrit Beaubourg.*

CHAPTER 1

The Poet and His Age

I *Biography*

FRANCIS Ponge was born on 27 March 1899 in Montpellier, close to the Mediterranean in the old French province of Languedoc. His father, Armand Ponge, was a local branch manager for the National Discount Bank of Paris, but in 1900 he was moved to a post in Avignon, on the Rhône, where he and his family stayed until 1909. The Ponge family had roots going back over the centuries in the Mediterranean region, as was also the case of the family of Juliette Saurel, François's mother.

Ponge was not left untouched by his early experience of the particular qualities of the Southern French geography. If his poetry often moves in the realms of the fluid and the viscous, it also reflects the sharpness of light and contour which he would have come to know as a child in the Midi. So, Ponge recreates the mimosa and the sun, angular stone and hard pebble, pine forests and silent lizards: "Il est certain que je suis une herbe ou une branchette, une feuille d'un arbre de ces régions, et que cela m'a déterminé."[1] ("It is clear that I am a plant, a small branch, a leaf from one of the trees of those regions, and that this has shaped me").

It appears that Ponge manifested during his early childhood an interest in and a talent for music, one particular artistic disposition which perhaps is not too evident in his work. On his own admission, though, music preoccupied him well before he thought of turning to words as his mode of expression: "Bien que je n'en aie pas écrit un seul mot encore, la musique, pendant toute ma jeunesse, fut mon principal moyen d'expression, tandis que je ne pense pas avoir composé une seule poésie avant le printemps de 1915"[2] ("Although I had not written a single word up until then, music was my principal means of expression during all my youth, while I cannot remember having written a single poem before the Spring of 1915").

17

Following another change of job, Armand Ponge took his family to Caen, in Normandy, in 1909, and the clarity and sharp definition of the South were thus replaced by the vague, more grey softness of the North. Francis Ponge was sent to the *lycée* in Caen which bore the name of the writer—Malherbe—whom he was to come to admire and to write about. Here, Ponge received an education which included two broad areas of great importance for his poetry, namely classical Greek and Latin on the one hand, and natural sciences on the other. His classical background led him later to develop a sustained interest in linguistic concision and density, and to try to restore to French the strength and depth he thought it had once gained from Latin, especially from such writers as Lucretius and Tacitus; while the apparently dispassionate and closely observed presentation of the world of objects—which constitutes one of the important bases on which Ponge's work is founded—could be said to reveal a scientifically inclined sensibility.

In 1913, at the age of fourteen, Ponge traveled through England, Belgium, and Holland in the company of his uncle, a teacher at the Lycée Condorcet. Subsequently, back in school, Ponge showed his fast-evolving literary abilities by obtaining high grades and by coming out first in his class in the baccalaureate dissertation. His tastes in reading at this time were at once surprising and predictable. He read the symbolists, including Kahn and Merrill, but found distasteful the Gide of *Paludes* and of the *Nourritures terrestres*, whose feebleness and cloudiness he considered especially displeasing.

A third major period in Ponge's life began in 1916 when he left Caen and settled in Paris, at his grandmother's house. He entered the preparatory class ("Hypokhâgne") at the Lycée Louis-le-Grand for entry into the Grandes Écoles. However, his progress toward his final educational goal of a place in the École Normale Supérieure was checked on two occasions, respectively in 1918 and in the following year, by a distressing and apparently inexplicable physical inability to speak during the oral examination. This would appear to have been part of a more general crisis which Ponge suffered at that time, during which his self-confidence became severely undermined.

However, it was during this period that Ponge began to become politically aware and to commit himself to the Left. The Russian Revolution struck him as being potentially of more significance in the long term than the Great War, and this might be allied to his broad concern, shown both directly and obliquely in his writing, with the relationship of the individual and society, and the power of the latter over the former. In 1917, he inveighed against a "société hideuse de débauche,"[3] in which we may see, mirroring as it does his wider attitude, an element of youthful rebelliousness, a disgust with the coarsening and corrupting effect of society, and a reaction to the particular circumstances of the so-called "war-to-end-all-wars." Like the dadaists and the surrealists, to the second of which groups he was later briefly and tenuously joined, Ponge knew the mixture of despair and revolt in the face of an ideologically lame world, which was what was left when the fighting stopped. Ponge's nascent literary ideas during the war years seem to have evolved around the premise that, at the same time as refusing to compromise with a moribund social order, he would have nothing to do with the literature which was this order's mouthpiece. One critic, Jean Thibaudeau, has suggested that Ponge's crisis of speechlessness mentioned above might be explained in terms of his choking back, internalizing a very real cry of horror and revolt in the face of the catastrophe of the war.[4]

In 1918, Ponge was mobilized in the infantry at Falaise. The resultant experience of military life proved disastrous; it reinforced his mounting and somewhat political feelings of revolt against the classes which determined the nature of society, and which, spiritually dead and bombastic in tone, had the power to silence individuals of character. On the positive side, however, while still in the army, Ponge was able, in the summer of 1919, to strike up a friendship with two important men of letters, Jean Hytier and Gabriel Audisio.

In September 1919, Ponge was demobilized, and soon made his way back to Paris where he became an habitué of the Left Bank café circles. It is from this time that Ponge's emergence as a poet dates. In 1922 he published a few poems in *Le Mouton Blanc*, a review started by friends from the École Normale, and whose guiding spirit was Hytier. Ponge's own work soon came to the attention of the *Nouvelle Revue Française* and its editor Jacques Rivière, to whom Ponge sent a few poems grouped under the title of *Les Trois satires*. At the same time, Ponge met the distinguished man of letters, Jean Paulhan. His encounter with the literary world of Paris left Ponge disgusted, however. He disliked the insincerity he found there, and refused to make the moves necessary for self-advancement.

In 1923, Armand Ponge died, and the poet's widowed mother then came to live in Paris, in an apartment which she shared with her son. Quickly, Ponge became burdened with financial difficulties, to relieve which he took a secretarial post in the Gallimard publishing house. Again, Ponge's hostility to the established world of letters welled up in him, and his undisguised contempt for the literary cliques with whom he had to deal led him to resign his job: "j'avais envie, à chaque instant, d'envoyer mon encrier à la figure de monsieur Cocteau ou de monsieur je ne sais plus qui, au lieu de prendre ses instructions pour la fabrication de ses livres..."[5] ("I wanted all the time to throw my inkwell in Monsieur Cocteau's face, or in monsieur such-and-such's face, instead of taking their instructions about the publication of their books...). Ponge seems to have dedicated, in the 1920's, to a long and perhaps ill-formulated process of finding an aesthetic which would serve his spirit of revolt. He later spoke of his wish at that time to construct some sort of bomb—secret, and devastating in its effects once it exploded.[6] During this period, Ponge published infrequently; a few pieces in *Commerce*, in the *Nouvelle Revue Française*, and in the first number of *Le Surréalisme au service de la révolution*. He continued to frequent the Latin Quarter cafés as well as seeing Paulhan and the German-born philosopher Groethuysen.

Perhaps in view of Ponge's evident mental turbulence at this time, it should not seem surprising that he suffered a nervous depression, from which he went to convalesce in Normandy. There, according to Philippe Sollers, he rediscovered the tonic effect of the sheer presence of the natural world: "C'est alors un véritable ravissement.... Après l'anti-chambre logique, voici le tonique extérieur. Les choses sont là..."[7] ("This is the time of a veritable enchantment.... After the antechamber of logic, here is the tonic of the exterior world. Things are there..."). Appropriately, Ponge, in revolt against language, literature, and institutions, became involved, albeit at the periphery, with the surrealist movement, whose heyday was during the 1920s. In the last two years or so of that decade, Ponge participated in some of the movement's activities, was interested in the kind of investigations it was undertaking, yet kept his distance from the more flamboyant displays of surrealist orthodoxy. He frequented *Le Cyrano*, a café favored by Breton, Éluard, and Aragon, and was present at the gatherings which took place in Breton's home in the rue de la Fontaine. However, seemingly for financial reasons, Ponge left the surrealist group prior to his marriage, in July 1931, to Odette Chabanel. He needed a steady source of income, and to this end he took a job with

Messageries Hachette, with whom he was to remain until 1937, despite the growing frustrations and wretchedness brought about by his experience with that company. In a text written during these years, "R. C. Seine No.," Ponge gives a glimpse of the atmosphere which prevailed there: "C'est par un escalier de bois jamais ciré depuis trente ans, dans la poussière des mégots jetés à la porte, au milieu d'un peloton de petits employés à la fois mesquins et sauvages, en chapeau melon, leur valise à soupe à la main, que deux fois par jour commence notre asphyxie"[8] ("It is via a staircase which has not seen polish for thirty years, in the filth of cigarette butts dropped in the doorway, in the midst of a squad of little employees who are at the same time petty and unsociable, in their bowler hats, clutching their lunch boxes, that our twice-daily asphyxiation begins"). While this is undistinguished prose, it does demonstrate something of Ponge's social and political position, a kind of horrified sympathy for his fellow workers which culminated in his becoming a trade-union official in the Confédération Générale du Travail (CGT), playing a prominent part in a sit-in strike at Hachette, and finally in his being dismissed from his job in 1937. He had joined the Communist party earlier that year, arguing that not to take sides politically was in effect a decision to opt for one side, the bad one in fact. He therefore chose the least bad. The Communist party appeared to him the only one with an effective grasp of syndicalist questions. Echoing, perhaps, some of the surrealists' soul-searching political debate of the late 1920s and early 1930s, Ponge decided that man's total condition, his mental as much as his physical life, could change for the better only if his social situation did too. Ponge put his time and energy into his union activities and his job, for the time it still had to last, as well as into his family life. As a result, he was left with very little time in which to do his writing, a mere twenty minutes an evening, as he has said.[9] Yet these were the days when Ponge was at work on those carefully constructed prose poems through which he has come to be known as the "poet of things," and which were to be published in 1942 with the title *Le Parti pris des choses*, an ambiguous title which will be discussed later.

Between his leaving Hachette and the outbreak of World War II, Ponge was more or less unemployed, although he did some work in the insurance business. On mobilization, he was sent to Rouen, only to be demobilized in 1940. He subsequently moved down to Roanne, in the Loire *département*, where he set up in insurance.

During his time there, he began to write the critical and creative pieces which were later to be collected together under the title of *La Rage de l'expression.*

In the domain of his political activities, Ponge established links with the Communist-based Front National in 1941, and he sheltered some of its leading members in his house. He next moved on to Lyons, one of the principal centers of the Resistance movement, and joined the editorial staff of the newspaper *Progrès de Lyon,* becoming its regional editor at Bourg-en-Bresse during 1942. He also became the political representative for the *Comité des Journalistes* in the unoccupied Southern zone of France, with the purpose of organizing and rallying the journalists in that area. After the Germans had taken over the unoccupied zone, in November 1942, and *Progrès* had voluntarily closed itself down, Ponge withdrew, in February 1943, to Coligny, a village in the Ain. From there, he maintained his double roles of active Resistance worker and practicing poet. In fact, the war years were of significance for Ponge the writer. Not only was *Le Parti pris des choses* published then, but Ponge was in contact with Audisio, with the prominent literary figure Pascal Pia, and, through the latter, with Camus, who in 1956 was to write an important critique of the poet. Furthermore, it was during the war years that Sartre wrote what remains one of the most penetrating evaluations of Ponge's poetry, triggered by his reading of *Le Parti pris des choses,* and published first in *Poésie 44,* and later as part of *Situations I* (1947), with the title "L'Homme et les choses."

After the Liberation, Ponge returned to Paris where he took up Aragon's offer of the post of literary and art editor of the Communist weekly *Action.* His period with *Action* (to 1946) was fruitful for Ponge in terms of the literary and artistic stimulus he received. *Action* published texts by Aragon, Éluard, Paulhan, Char, Queneau, Sartre, Audisio, and others, while at the same time Ponge was meeting painters such as Picasso, Fautrier, Braque, and Dubuffet, who were to inspire many of his essays in *Le Peintre à l'étude* (1948).

In 1946 Ponge gave up his editorship on *Action* because of an ideological clash; he could not accept certain doctrinaire attitudes toward art which the journal and Communist orthodoxy had adopted. On top of this, he decided in 1947 not to renew his membership of the Communist party. There now began a difficult period for Ponge and his family, who had to live for some years in very considerable poverty. He was forced, for example, to sell some of his books and furniture to settle tax debts. He managed to struggle on, making ends meet through what he earned from lecture engagements and occasional publications, usually of limited luxury editions. The late 1940s and early 1950s reduced Ponge to a state of depression reminiscent of the one he had suffered in the 1920s. His second book of poetry, *Proêmes*, appeared in 1948, to be followed by *La Seine* in 1950.

Only in 1952 did life become easier, when Ponge was employed by the Alliance Française as teacher-lecturer, a position which he was to hold for twelve years, until his retirement. His life during these years was divided between his teaching, writing, and lecture tours abroad. *La Rage de l'expression* appeared in 1952, and French radio broadcast an important and substantial conversation between Ponge, Breton, and Reverdy in the same year (later published in *Le Grand Recueil*). By the mid-1950s, Ponge was becoming somewhat better known, thanks to the *NLF*'s "Hommage à Francis Ponge" number of September 1956. Nevertheless, his published works remained relatively small in number and difficult to obtain, while one of his major projects, a book on Malherbe, failed to interest a publisher, and in fact appeared only in 1965, and then not quite in the form originally envisaged. In his family life, the 1950s saw the death of Ponge's mother (1954), and the marriage of his daughter Armande (1957). Ponge's lecture tours took him principally to various cities in Belgium and Germany, as well as around France, and the uneven decade of the 1950s closed with his visit to Capri in September 1959, to receive a poetry prize, and with the conferment on him of the Légion d'honneur two months later.

The 1960s opened more auspiciously. Material worries receded considerably, and on the proceeds from the sale of some paintings, Ponge was able to buy, in 1961, a farmhouse at Bar-sur-Loup, in Provence. Furthermore, his reputation as an important poet grew significantly at about this time. He was the subject of a lecture which Sollers gave at the Sorbonne in 1960, and Ponge himself entered into negotiations with Gallimard about the publication of a large-scale book, which appeared in 1961 with the title *Le Grand Recueil*, and which comprised three volumes (entitled *Lyres*, *Méthodes*, and *Pièces*), containing most of what Ponge had written up to that date. It is fair to say that it was this book which really made Ponge, if not a household name, certainly one which became known to a wide section of the reading public. Volume 1 was composed largely of essays on painters and the fine arts, volume 2 of his theoretical writings about poetry, while in the third were gathered creative texts, including many examples of those "thing-centered" poems to which Ponge principally owes his reputation. It should be pointed out that these texts had already begun to interest the scholars and critics who have come to be known as the *Tel Quel* group. When their linguistics-based review of the same name brought out its first issue in 1960, it contained a poem by Ponge, "La figue sèche." This review has since published other texts by Ponge, as well as three articles to date about his work. By championing Ponge, putting him under the fashionable spotlight of linguistical and semiological scrutiny, *Tel Quel* has assured him a degree of fame and notoriety, taking further the publicity begun by Sartre's article and Camus's open letter.

There have been other important works by Ponge published since *Le Grand Recueil*, though the latter remains his most substantial. A large single volume called, paradoxically, *Tome premier*, came out in 1965 and included *Le Parti pris des choses*. The same year saw at last the publication of the book on Malherbe, definitively entitled *Pour un Malherbe*, a collection of somewhat disorganized and repetitive chapters and notes, originally intended for publication in the *Écrivains de toujours* series, as well as for various separate articles and broadcasts. In the following year, Ponge was a visiting professor at Columbia University. Following that appointment in 1967 Ponge published two more books, *Nouveau Recueil* and *Le Savon*, both mixtures of creative and critical texts. Also in that year, a discussion between Ponge and Sollers was broadcast on French radio and was published in book form in 1970. In 1971, *La Fabrique du Pré* appeared, a compendium of the notes, drafts, and revisions which all led up to the definitive version of Ponge's poem "Le pré."

In 1973, Ponge received the Ingram Merrill Foundation International Prize (for 1972), and this success was followed by a similar one in 1974, when he obtained the Books Abroad Neustadt International Literary Prize. Where the 1960s had been a decade of production and publicity, the 1970s has been one of recognition and respectability. In 1975, a large-scale colloquium on "Ponge inventeur et classique" was held at the International Cultural Centre at Cerisy-la-Salle. The proceedings of this colloquium were published in 1977. Also in 1977, two more books came out: *Comment une figue de paroles et pourquoi*, another collection of notes and drafts, this time of the poem *La figue sèche*, and constituting, like *La Fabrique du Pré*, a permanent record of work in progress; and *L'Atelier contemporain*, a further contribution to Ponge's writings about the fine arts. An exhibition of his manuscripts and books, and of paintings in some way connected with him, was held at the Centre Georges Pompidou, Paris, from 25 February to 4 April 1977.

Currently, Ponge is living quietly in Provence. It would seem that he is not in the best of health; in 1977, he had to decline an invitation to talk to an audience at the Cardiff campus of the University of Wales. At the time of writing (spring 1978), Ponge's most recent publication is an article entitled "Nous, mots français," in *NRF* for 1 March 1978.

II *Shaping Forces and Affinities*

It will be apparent from the foregoing that Ponge has aroused the interest of certain prominent literary figures whose aesthetics and ideologies vary considerably one from another. Sartre, for example, was fascinated by Ponge in 1944, just as Breton had been welcoming fifteen years previously, yet of course Sartre's whole view of the world is fundamentally in conflict with that of Breton—the materialist Sartre has written very antagonistically about the surrealists' transcendental enterprise. Similarly, the heritage of literary influences revealed overtly and more discreetly by Ponge brings together apparently ill-assorted names. He devotes the whole of a laudatory book to the austerely classical poet Malherbe, while claiming some affinity with two poets of the late nineteenth century, both luminaries of the delirious extreme of romanticism, Rimbaud and Lautréamont.

Where does Ponge stand in terms of the traditions in French literature, and what in particular is his alignment in his own century? Answers to these questions belong more to the end of this study, but what immediately seems to be clear is that Ponge, owing some allegiance to disparate writers and schools, adopted by men of letters and critics of varied and clashing ideologies, stands on his own, defying satisfactory classification. The critic Marcel Raymond, in his seminal *De Baudelaire au surréalisme*, has traced the development of twentieth-century French poetry up to the time of World War II along two separate lines, both derivative of the watershed that was Baudelaire, and which he calls the "artiste" and the "voyant" lines. The former includes such names as Mallarmé and

Valéry, the latter Rimbaud, and the surrealists. It is problematical, and possibly unprofitable, to try to attach Ponge firmly to either one of these two lines. His declaration of interest in Rimbaud and his participation in surrealism ought to make him a twentieth-century believer in "voyance"; but a reading of his creative work, and more particularly of several of his theoretical pieces, reveals a Mallarmean bias in his aesthetic. Yet Ponge is hostile to Valéry, Mallarmé's most important inheritor in this century. Then, Ponge's active involvement in the surrealist movement (he contributed a short article entitled "Plus-que-raisons" to the first issue of *Le Surréalisme au service de la révolution*, as well as signing a protest letter about the French army's handling of one of the surrealist group's members, following what the army had taken to be his insulting behavior) seems puzzling.

While the movement's self-given role as the scourge of complacent thinking and bourgeois manners must have appealed to the political, angry Ponge of the 1920s, surrealism's attitudes to art and aesthetics apparently bear no resemblance to Ponge's. It is frankly difficult to see what affinity there can be between a doctrine which preaches automatism, the spontaneous disgorging of semiwaking fantasy, and the works of Ponge, which have always been controlled, measured, linguistically self-conscious to the point of preciosity in their frequent use of conceit and wit. Ponge's writings, whether prose poems about packing-crates, lengthy defenses of Malherbe, or involved theorizing about the objective status of language itself, are unified by their axiomatic view that language is something which occurs consciously and deliberately. It is as necessary to man, as non-contingent as the slime which it secretes is to the snail, as Ponge writes in one of his poems. Language expresses man and the world which his gaze discloses, not in a syntactically and grammatically anarchic form, as was the case with surrealism in its first phase, but, in total opposition to this, it does so in resolutely ordered and precise structures of syntax. This has to be because syntax is not so much a useful if contingent convention as a necessary, intrinsic part of man, the distinctive quality which defines him. Man, Ponge often seems to be saying, is his language. In some ways, surrealism shared this view; but, because it fleshed it out with an idiom which, as well as being so often uncontrolled, was basically a late flourishing of a romantic approach to language, it becomes unprofitable to seek to elucidate Ponge's kind of writing in terms of a presumed surrealist guidance.

Other alignments seem more possible. If Ponge has learned some lessons about classical form and measure from Malherbe, he resembles another classical writer, La Fontaine, in that his poems often have the quality of fables. Indeed, this very quality allies him to a much more recent writer, Jules Renard, a contemporary of Rimbaud and Lautréamont, whose *Histoires naturelles* (1896) have the same mixture of accurate observation, powerful evocation, and gentle irony as is found in a good deal of Ponge's work.

However, to judge by the orientation of a lot of the more interesting and convincing criticism about Ponge, his alignment is more with contemporary traditions which combine literature and philosophy. Camus has written of Ponge's work in terms of his own absurdist notions about the nonsignificance of the world, while Sartre has linked Ponge to phenomenology. Inasmuch as Ponge's work posits a discontinuity between man and a universe indifferent to him, Camus's observations are pertinent; inasmuch as Ponge never frees himself of the straitjacket of an anthropocentric understanding of the world, even though his poems seem to be about objects as "things-in-themselves," Sartre's concept of Ponge's "phenomenology of nature" is illuminating. Neither approach, however, can fully reveal the mechanism of Ponge's poetic structures (although Sartre's does appear to come close). It should be stated at the beginning that out of the range and complexity of the philosophy of phenomenology, it is the aspect of the phenomenology of perception which has relevance for a study of Ponge. It could even be said that phenomenology's insistence on the subject-object fusion ("reality" amounts to how the "objective" world appears to human consciousness) is this philosophy's most helpful contribution in elucidating Ponge's work. But it is a highly significant contribution and penetrates to the core of Ponge's method. Interestingly, a knowledge of Sartre's novel *La Nausée* (1938), and of some parts of it in particular, is appropriate to a study of Ponge. The way in which Sartre's protagonist Roquentin undergoes a crisis in how he perceives and understands the world, whose appearances he can no longer codify and make safe for himself, prefigures Ponge's method of perception. Roquentin and Ponge both seem to be exercised by the problem of deciding whether the phenomenal world is grammatical or agrammatical, to borrow the vocabulary of Arthur Danto in his book on Sartre.[10]

Lastly, and to some extent consequent on his position vis-à-vis phenomenological methods, Ponge's work might be cautiously aligned with the "nouveau roman" in France. Robbe-Grillet has written some interesting pages about Ponge in his apologia for the new novel, entitled *Pour un nouveau roman* (1963). The linking factor between this controversial new style in fiction and Ponge's work again seems to be phenomenology. Robbe-Grillet rejects the traditional mode of the omniscient narrator, actual or implied, in complete charge of the novel, a mode favored by Balzac, whom Robbe-Grillet gives as an example. This sort of writing has its supports rooted in the unquestioned control of the author over the psychology of his characters. When Balzac makes his characters act, decide, choose, it is accepted that he knows absolutely the inner reaches of those characters' strengths and weaknesses, and is uniquely responsible for them. Robbe-Grillet refuses all access to "inside knowledge" and instead says that the writer must be more honest and accept that all that which he has to go on, all that which literally he can know, is the behavior, the activity of his characters, and not their motivation. Hence the apparently disjointed, inconsequential writing so often found in the new novel, with its deliberate lack of the vocabulary of cause and effect, of explanations of events; hence, too, the paucity of conjunctions, adjectives, and adverbs. By contrast, the events in these books are seen in terms of gesture and description. In other words, the novels are built of data taken without direct comment from the external world. They are literally about how things appear, how they are registered in consciousness. They appear factual, and are so, in that they display two conditions of a fact, first, an event in the world, and second, a human perception of that event. They are, in short, phenomenological accounts of experience, just as Ponge's poems are very often phenomenological re-creations of objects.[11]

Such, then, are the factors and forces which may be said to have helped shape Ponge's poetics. They are varied, and some of them appear to be strangely assorted, if not incompatible. To revert to Marcel Raymond's thesis of the two poetic traditions since Baudelaire, it might be just possible to place Ponge in the "artiste" as opposed to the "voyant" camp. The single most telling reason for this judgment would be that Ponge shares with the foremost poet of the "artiste" tradition, Mallarmé, the view that language is autonomous, pure "logos." To the limited extent that one can put Ponge within any tradition, he might be said to be a classical (more than a romantic), a Mallarmean (more than a Rimbaldian) writer whose greatest achievements have been realized under the not-too-distant sign of phenomenology.

III   *Words as Poems: Words about Poems*

The three-part division of Ponge's *Le Grand Recueil* accurately reflects his major preoccupations as writer and thinker. Consistently he has been concerned with writing poems, with writing about writing poems, and with the fine arts. Of these concerns, the last will receive no treatment in this study, as an appreciation of Ponge as art critic properly belongs elsewhere.

A distinctive feature of Ponge the poet is that he has written probably as much, if not more, about the processes of writing as he has written poems. Theory and practice are equally important. Sometimes the two are kept distinct, but at other times Ponge writes texts which mesh these two aspects together, and make them seem the constituents of a single unity. *La Rage de l'expression*, in particular the section entitled "Le Carnet du bois de pins," may be seen as a prominent example of this technique.

Having alluded to the individualistic, "thing-centered" quality of much of Ponge's poetry, it is now appropriate to quote in full a text which encapsulates this quality. The most pertinent are generally to be found in *Le Parti pris des choses*, from which the following, "Le pain," is taken:

La surface du pain est merveilleuse d'abord à cause de cette impression quasi panoramique qu'elle donne: comme si l'on avait à sa disposition sous la main les Alpes, le Taurus ou la Cordillère des Andes.
Ainsi donc une masse amorphe en train d'éructer fut glissée pour nous dans le four stellaire, où durcissant elle s'est façonnée en vallées, crêtes, ondulations, crevasses.... Et tous ces plans dès lors si nettement articulés, ces dalles minces où la lumière avec application couche ses feux,—sans un regard pour la mollesse ignoble sous-jacente.
Ce lâche et froid sous-sol que l'on nomme la mie a son tissu pareil à celui des éponges: feuilles ou fleurs y sont comme des soeurs siamoises soudées par tous les coudes à la fois. Lorsque le pain rassit ses fleurs fanent et se rétrécissent: elles se détachent alors les unes des autres, et la masse en devient friable....
Mais brisons-la: car le pain doit être dans notre bouche moins objet de respect que de consommation. [12]

The surface of bread is marvellous firstly because of the almost panoramic impression which it gives: as if one had ready for use the Alps, the Taurus range or the Andean Belt.
Thus an amorphous eructating mass was slid for us into the stellar oven where, as it hardened, it became valleys, crests, undulations, crevices....
And all those planes henceforth so clearly linked, those slender slabs where

the light sinks its fires with concentration—without any attention to the ignoble softness underneath.

That slack and cold subsoil which is called the crumb has a fabric which is like that of sponges: leaves and flowers exist there like Siamese sisters joined together by all their elbows at once. When bread becomes stale these flowers fade away and shrink: they then break away one from the other, and the mass becomes crumbly...

But let's break off here: for bread should be, in our mouth, less an object of our respect than of consumption.

> (*T*, 51; Francis Ponge, *Tome premier*, Éditions Gallimard;
> translated by Martin Sorrell)

This typifies the more successful, tightly organized, verbally precise and sophisticated work about objects, of which Ponge is often capable. The reader encountering Ponge for the first time might well ask whether this is a poem at all—Ponge, incidentally, on the whole refuses to call his creations "poems," as shown by his coinage of "proême"—and whether it is not simply a description couched in original terms. In answer to the second question, the claim that "Le pain" is just description of bread is not sufficient.[13] It may appear to be so because it concentrates entirely on saying something about bread, and its form looks unpoetical, factual, like a short and organized piece of prose. But anyone called upon to give a straightforward description of bread to someone who did not know what it was would surely not produce Ponge's text, or anything like it. In fact, "Le pain" is built on the assumption that everyone knows bread well and can describe it for themselves. It leaves description behind to say something else. What it is trying to say relates to the first objection suggested above, namely, that it is not a poem. Ponge has shifted his focus from a description of bread (though not from an evocation of it) to an exploration of its linguistic correlates. He is examining the possibilities of language not in its role of *describing* a thing (where language is used as a conventional sign symbolizing something apart from itself in the real world), but in its supposed capacity to *be* that thing. This is an ambitious and perhaps unclear program, and needs to be discussed more fully in a later chapter.

But the fact that Ponge is trying to create, in heightened language, texts which are autonomous, and intended to be as detached and solid as objects, indeed objects in themselves, situates his work in a poetic world, and not a world of prose. What the program largely hinges on is the notion, which Ponge first puts forward in *Méthodes* (20), of "adéquation," of which there are examples in "Le pain." This is an ideal condition (to be arrived at by particular procedures) in which the verbal representation of a thing is intended to be so close to the thing itself that it partakes of it, becomes, if possible, that thing. This may operate at the level of individual words or of the overall structure of the whole poem, or both. On the way to "adéquation" the poet may have to use various metaphorical ways of rendering reality; he will also have recourse to a considerable amount of wordplay, including puns. "Adéquation" in the context of Ponge's work will be satisfactorily described only with the help of examples, but it may be loosely translated as "equivalence," and summarily defined as the congruence of object and language.

Thus, in "Le pain," the overall structure of the poem shows "adéquation" in its progression from surface to interior, from crust to crumb, in its temporal progression from the bread freshly baked to its becoming stale, finally in the climactic "brisons-la," meaning "let us break it," that is, the bread, in order to eat it; but, through a pun ("brisons là"), it can mean "let us stop all this talk." Ponge is saying, in the poem's last paragraph, that the condition, or definition, of bread is that it should be eaten; it exists for this alone, its consumption is the definitive part of its being. Therefore, the poem, having first been physically present on the page, like a loaf of bread on the table, must, also exactly like bread, be consumed (and consummated, as there is a pun on "consommation") and disappear. Poem and bread alike reach their necessary and paradoxical end by ceasing to be. "Adéquation" is thus achieved, and may be seen as one way of defining the impetus to narrow down, possibly to close, the gap between form and content.

Let us now turn to Ponge's repeated device of writing about the writing of poems. This occurs in many cases within a text which also contains the very poem he is writing about. At other times, more subtly, it turns out that the "theoretical" discussion is an integral part of the poetic text. Examples of these procedures are plentiful but generally too long to be quoted here (one such is "Le Carnet du bois de pins"). However, an extract from "Le mimosa" is sufficiently self-contained to form a satisfactory illustration. It is taken from the early part of this long piece:

Je ne choisis pas les sujets les plus faciles: voilà pourquoi je choisis le mimosa. Comme c'est un sujet très difficile il faut donc que j'ouvre un cahier.

Tout d'abord, il faut noter que le mimosa ne m'inspire pas du tout. Seulement, j'ai une idée de lui au fond de moi qu'il faut que j'en sorte parce

que je veux en tirer profit. Comment se fait-il que le mimosa ne m'inspire
pas du tout—alors qu'il a été l'une de mes adorations, de mes prédilections
enfantines? Beaucoup plus que n'importe quelle autre fleur, il me donnait de
l'émotion. Seul de toutes il me passionnait. Je doute si ce ne serait pas par le
mimosa qu'a été éveillée ma sensualité, si elle ne s'est pas éveillée aux soleils
du mimosa. Sur les ondes puissantes de son parfum je flottais, extasié. Si
bien qu'à présent le mimosa, chaque fois qu'il apparaît dans mon intérieur,
à mon entour, me rappelle tout cela et fane aussitôt.

Il faut donc que je remercie le mimosa. Et puisque j'écris, il serait
inadmissible qu'il n'y ait pas de moi un écrit sur le mimosa.

Mais vraiment, plus je tourne autour de cet arbuste, plus il me paraît que
j'ai choisi un sujet difficile. C'est que j'ai un très grand respect pour lui, que
je ne voudrais pas le traiter à la légère (étant donné surtout son extrême
sensibilité). Je ne veux l'approcher qu'avec délicatesse.... [14]

I don't choose the easiest subjects: that's why I choose the mimosa. As it's so
difficult a subject I must therefore open a notebook.

First of all, I must note down that the mimosa doesn't inspire me at all.
Only, I've got an idea about it deep inside me and I must get beyond it so
that I may gain something from it. How is it that the mimosa doesn't inspire
me at all—when it was one of my most adored things, one of my
predilections as a child? Much more than any other flower, it aroused my
emotions. Alone, it captivated me. I doubt whether it would not be the
mimosa which awakened my sensuality, whether my sensuality was not
awakened by the suns of the mimosa. On the powerful waves of its perfume
I floated, enraptured. So that now, the mimosa, every time it appears in my
house, or around me, reminds me of all that and immediately fades.

I must therefore thank the mimosa. And, as I write, it can't be that I
shouldn't write a piece about the mimosa.

But really, the more I go around this shrub, the more it seems to me that
I've chosen a difficult subject. What it is, is that I've a very great respect for
it and wouldn't want to treat it rashly (given above all its extreme
sensitivity). I want to approach it only with the greatest care....

This can and must be taken at two levels. Firstly, Ponge is making a
direct statement, as he apparently stands back from the poetic text
proper, about the difficulty he is meeting as he grapples with his
subject matter. To this extent, the extract seems to be a kind of
footnote in prose to a poem which presumably occurs elsewhere in
the text of "Le mimosa." Yet, in reality, it is footnote and poetic text
at the same time. For, at the second level, it becomes apparent that
Ponge is saying considered, carefully phrased, evocative things
about the mimosa. He conveys with a certain force the sensory
reactions which he and many people share when in its presence. This

is conveyed principally in the second paragraph. The last paragraph, however, adds a further dimension to the evocation of the mimosa; it becomes clear that this extended, digressive "footnote" is in fact a subtle poetic text which is operating on the basis of "adéquation." The subject of the mimosa, Ponge says, is a difficult one, because he cannot quite get hold of it; nor must he be too casual about it. Why not? Not simply because he will show himself to be an inept writer, but because the mimosa itself will be at risk, the mimosa itself cannot be taken hold of, except at the peril of crushing it through lack of gentleness and care ("délicatesse"). Subject (mimosa) and verbal representation (the poem about it) are implicitly one and the same thing. Ponge steers his text toward this position by beginning the last paragraph with the idea, a conceit of sorts, that he is "turning around the shrub," that is, he is finding it difficult to seize hold of the flower, with its delicacy and its evanescent perfume, and of the poem, with its problems of linguistic accuracy.

The two extracts examined in this chapter are intended as pointers to the major areas of Ponge's concern—the writing of poems, and the elaboration, either within the poems or separately, of his literary theory and method. The last mentioned, often lucid and informative, sometimes long-winded, self-satisfied and repetitive, can throw light on the former. It is the poems themselves which remain Ponge's most important contribution to literature, and, although some are overwritten and ordinary, like his theoretical pieces, there is surely no doubt that Ponge has created a unique and masterly poetic diction in a number of those texts, limpid yet dense, which so often have the deceptive appearance of mere descriptions.

To take up a point made in the previous section, Ponge is one of those poets who have written as much about poetry and poetics as they have actual poems. A peculiarity of Ponge is that, while his theoretical material often remains quite distinct from his poems, nonetheless a significant proportion of his texts are at once what can loosely be termed creative and theoretical. That is, they set out to be poetic texts on a specific subject which Ponge has chosen, and, in achieving this poetic status, and perhaps *in order* to achieve it, they incorporate the verbalized thought processes, as it were the stepping-stones, which make evident the successive stages, with their difficulties, their failures, and their victories, through which Ponge has passed on the way to his final text. Traditionally, we expect such annotations and tentative formulations to remain extrinsic to what we conceive of as a finished and polished piece of writing. With

Ponge, this is not always so; while he is readily thought of as the poet of objects, in fact he is not primarily concerned to be a modern disciple of the nineteenth-century Parnassian desire to have the author eclipse himself from his works. Ponge is certainly a poet of objects, his raw material is predominantly the nonhuman world, but he never loses sight of his position as one human being, principally in his capacity as manipulator of language, face to face with the data of the external world. Hence one interesting characteristic of Ponge's published work, which is that, on occasions, the notes made toward definitive poetic texts, notes clearly extrinsic to these texts, have been published separately. This is perhaps a predictable if idiosyncratic feature in a poet who views language and writing in the way Ponge does. Thus, *Comment une figue de paroles et pourquoi*, the 1977 publication of the manuscript fragments, sketches, etc. of the poem "La figue sèche" of 1959; thus also, *La Fabrique du Pré* (1971), which falls into the same category.

Therefore, a tripartite division can be made among the works of Ponge, and may be categorized as, first, the theoretical pieces, second, theoretical and creative texts combined in one, and, third, purely creative or poetic texts, those which most closely approximate to a traditional concept of the autonomous work of art. An investigation of Ponge's theories, as revealed principally by the first two of these categories, is the initial task to be undertaken. As an aid to this task, a useful distinction can be made between Ponge's poetic *theory* and his poetic *method*. It is not that these conflict with each other, rather that the latter extends the former, and introduces certain critical ideas and vocabulary which are not spelled out in the restricted area of abstraction and speculation. Both theory and method will be examined, and this will be followed by analysis of texts of the autonomous, poetic sort.

Given that Ponge does not seem to advance or unfold his arguments volume by volume, but goes over instead the same preoccupations, exemplifying repeatedly and repetitively the same aesthetic issues, a chronological approach to his work has no particular recommendation. Such an approach will therefore be replaced by a synthetic-analytical one.

CHAPTER 2

Poetic Theory

A FTER this opening survey of some of the more salient features of Ponge's work, a detailed consideration of the basis of theory provided for it by Ponge himself is necessary. The components of his poetics are usually interesting, sometimes illuminating, but occasionally pretentious and sententious.

I *False Languages*

Ponge begins the first in his book of essays on poetics, *Méthodes*, with a somewhat surprising and disingenuous claim: "Sans doute ne suis-je pas trés intelligent: en tout cas les idées ne sont pas mon fort"[1] ("No doubt I am not very intelligent: at any rate, ideas are not my strong point"). This particular essay, given the English title "My creative method," is one of Ponge's most important statements of his poetic faith. What he says about ideas is that they not only hold no interest for him, but that they also contravene the necessary laws of demarcation between the objective and the subjective. Ideas are invariably manifestations of one particular subjective, and too often they are passed off as objective, and, as such, as aspects of truth. Alluding to certain conventions of what is acceptable as poetic raw material, Ponge asks why it can be affirmed that curly blond hair is more *true* than straight dark hair, or that the nightingale's song is nearer the truth than the neighing of a horse. He claims that ideas are epiphenomenal. While he does not elaborate on this, in the context of his work the meaning seems to be that ideas are some kind of appended (and probably misleading) label deflecting the attention from the original phenomenon itself. There is here an echo of Kant's phrase about the "thing-in-itself" ("das Ding an sich"), also the idea of getting back to things themselves ("An die Sache selbst"), the starting point of phenomenology. The point of real substance which Ponge is making is not that all concern with ideas is valueless—as he himself recognizes, the very act of his writing the essay in which this issue is raised would be self-contradictory if this were so—but that it is not the place of the writer actually to supply ideas. Certainly, ideas may emerge from words, but "il n'en est pas moins bizarre pourtant d'exiger d'un écrivain des idées" ("yet it is not any less odd to demand ideas from a writer," *M*, 236). This in turn explains the more abstruse statement that words should not so much signify as function (*M*, 193), a statement which is supported in the following paragraph by the assertion, common enough in poetics but nevertheless problematical, that poets work with words and not with ideas.

Later (*M*, 231-35), Ponge does attempt to clarify this by means of an allegory in which he begins by stressing the master-craftsman condition of the poet—the fact that the poet works with the materials of words, in the way that the carpenter works with wood, or the jeweler with precious stones and metals—and then he points out that ideas as such do not enter into the act of creating furniture and jewelry.

Ponge goes on from this to elaborate the allegory of the tree by means of a kind of fable illustrating the primacy of words over ideas, though not before having conceded that it is too easy for the writer to let the words he is using slip away into the realm of ideas. In his fable, Ponge imagines that a tree has let its branches and leaves grow, and has inscribed certain abstract concepts on some of the leaves: "frankness," "lucidity," "love of trees," "good of trees," etc. This action, says Ponge, is authentic and sincere on the part of the tree, and all the other trees know this to be so. One day a woodcutter arrives and chops off one branch, which the tree considers a normal event. However, the tree becomes anxious when the woodcutter comes again to take off a second branch, as it notices that the ax handle is made out of the first branch. The tree's anxiety is justified, for the woodcutter now proceeds to chop down the whole tree. How should the tree react? Should it exclaim: "You as well, my son?" The situation, says Ponge, becomes tragic when the tree thinks: "So I am made of the wood which is used for axes" ("Je suis donc du bois dont on fait les haches," a rearrangement of the idiomatic expression "être du bois dont on fait les flûtes," indicating a person who can easily be led or manipulated).

The gist of Ponge's somewhat labored allegory seems to be that if one takes the artisan's raw materials—the carpenter's wood, the poet's words—and turns them into ideas, contrary to the interests of their unstated essences, in which Ponge must believe, then this action will be counterproductive and will destroy the very principles by which they came into existence. The tree, not resisting the threat to its condition of tree (its "tree-ness," its "en-soi," to use the Sartrean term), loses its authenticity and dies by its own hand, as it were, and through its own error. Similarly, language, the individual leaves and branches of words, wrongly inscribed with ideas, will be transformed into figurative ax handles, and their "word-ness" will also die. A belief inherent in this fable of the tree, and which is reiterated throughout Ponge's work, is that language used in poetry has an objective status, has the weight of a material substance existing independently of the writer, whose duty is to preserve and display to its best advantage this language in all its solidity. Although Ponge does not seek to eradicate himself from his creations, a fact mentioned earlier, nevertheless a guiding principle for him is that language is created but then released by man, and makes its subsequent way independently of him.

In *La Seine*, Ponge draws an analogy between formulated language and a stele: "il est naturel peut-être de concevoir un proverbe, voire n'importe quelle formule verbale et enfin n'importe quel livre comme une stèle, un monument, un roc, dans la mesure où il *s'oppose* aux pensées et à l'esprit..." ("it is perhaps natural to conceive of proverbs, indeed any verbal formula and ultimately any book as a stele, a monument, a rock insofar as it is in opposition to thoughts and mind...," *T*, 531). This belief in the substantiality of language, however interesting, begs questions of aesthetics, specifically those about the subjective ingredient in language, the place of metaphorical modes, and the role of imagination, a faculty which Ponge seems particularly to distrust.[2]

Superficially at least, it appears that Ponge has wanted to reject or possibly to modify these categories. As Ian Higgins points out in his valuable essay, Ponge has sought to leave behind the "flabby lyricism of much Symbolist and post-Symbolist poetry" while at the same time scorning the "indiscriminate welter of analogy" prevalent in modern poetry.[3] Undoubtedly, Ponge is hostile toward the romantic tradition in French verse. One of the traps of the romantic attitude is that language is shouted down by the more powerful voice of a subjective seeking to exhibit itself; language is brutalized and transcended. When the subjective is especially perverse or idiosyncratic, language risks being led into the most recondite areas of the hermetic. Yves Gohin has succinctly categorized these aspects of romanticism against which Ponge is reacting: "le maximum de spontanéité dans le maximum de subjectivité, et par conséquent le maximum d'hermétisme"[4] ("the maximum spontaneity in the maximum subjectivity, and consequently the maximum hermeticism"). Ponge himself has written that he likes the rule which corrects emotion (*P*, 310).

Romantic postures, subjective lyricism,[5] eloquence, the cult of ideas, all these lead to the abuse and then the ossification of language. It is as if Ponge had evolved his own version of Mallarmé's division of language into the vulgar, debased variety in everyday use, and the pristine, noncontingent absolute of purity, a division which Mallarmé establishes in "Le Tombeau d'Edgar Poe," where he declares in so many words his intention of rejecting the former in favor of the latter ("Donner un sens plus pur aux mots de la tribu"; "To give a purer sense to the language of the tribe"). The term which Ponge adopts for Mallarmé's tribal language is "manège," a word which can mean "trick" or "stratagem," but which, in Ponge's contexts, is more likely to have another of its meanings, "fairground roundabout." Ponge uses the word on a small but significant number of occasions. Each time, a pejorative quality is intended: "dans quel infime manège depuis des siècles tournent les paroles..." ("on what a paltry roundabout words have been turning for centuries...," *T*, 196); "le moindre soupçon de ronron poétique m'avertit seulement que je rentre dans le manège..." ("the least hint of the droning hum of poetry merely warns me that I'm back on the roundabout...," *T*, 258); "ce que je cherche, c'est à sortir de cet insipide manège dans lequel tourne l'homme..." ("what I want is to get off this insipid roundabout on which man turns...," *M*, 254); "une nouvelle image annule l'imagerie ancienne, fait sortir du manège..." ("a new image cancels old imagery, gets you off the roundabout...," *M*, 295).

The metaphor of the roundabout conveys Ponge's dissatisfaction with the vicious circle out of which the casual and disrespectful users of language cannot or do not seek to break. The "manège" is made up of complacency, laziness, habit, and too easily accepted convention. In the precise areas of his poetics, Ponge sees that the "manège" encrusts with layers of cliché, received ideas, and expression the objects which it is the poet's function to reveal in all their nakedness, in what Ponge would call all their reality. He singles out for special attack the image, an aspect of the metaphorical mode mentioned earlier. Images are welcome, says Ponge, if and when a fresh one can clear away a worn-out one. Yet

those things with which a poet is concerned have a healthy contempt
for the images, the lame linguistic categories, which get thrust upon
them: "Rien n'est plus réjouissant que la constante insurrection des
choses contre les images qu'on leur impose" ("Nothing is more
heartening than the constant rebellion of things against the images
imposed on them," *M*, 295-96). Things simply refuse to lie still in the
way demanded by imposed imagery.

The conclusion Ponge draws from his consideration of the
"manège," however, involves more than just a revitalization of
imagery. In the process of what he calls the removal of poetry's
disguises, he implies a more radical need for new subject matter,
presumably because the "manège" also comprises set attitudes about
what is acceptable material and what is not. If you want to jump off
the roundabout and slip away, then Ponge exhorts you to follow
him. It is simple, there is not far to go. Just consider a cigarette butt,
for example, or any object at all; the only true condition is to look at
it honestly, finally ("finalement"), with no regard for all the
irrelevancies uttered about man, about mind, to contemplate it
without shame ("sans vergogne," *M*, 254). A link with the methods
of phenomenology may be seen here. When Ponge asks us to
consider a cigarette, a Turkish towel, or whatever, not only is he
introducing apparently novel objects into the poetic repertoire, but
he is also commending a method of observation which calls to mind
the so-called "epoché," or "bracketing," of phenomena, as well as
the "eidetic reduction" of phenomenological investigation. These
concepts, deriving principally from Husserl, have to do with the
deliberate suspension of all habitual assumptions and beliefs about
the phenomena under examination; received opinions, all judgments,
even spatial and temporal facts, are set aside in the process of
"epoché," leaving the field clear for a confrontation with the
essential structure of the phenomenon. The act of describing what is
left goes hand in hand with the intuiting of that which is essential in
the phenomenon ("eidetic reduction"). Arguably, this activity is the
stuff of poetry; the process of "bracketing" is inherent in the act of
poetic creation.[6]

To reiterate something which was said in the introductory
chapter, Ponge writes many poems, such as "Le pain," which in one
sense are descriptions, but which seem also more than that. A
possible explanation of this ambivalence is that the poems indeed
are descriptions, aiming even to be definitions, of objects which
Ponge is subjecting to his own type of "bracketing" and "reduction."

It is possible to see "Le pain," and probably the majority of Ponge's texts, as ones in which presuppositions of all kinds, including most obviously linguistic ones, have been cast aside. Ponge elaborates on how this "bracketing" is to be done. Attention must be focused on the object exclusively and without fear or prejudice; it is of no use setting out to write about the cigarette butt only to abandon the task, or at least to lose proper focus, by becoming distracted by the fact that it is small in comparison to something else. Once this happens, you have sold out as a poet, you are once more ensnared in the "ronron" of the "manège" (*M*, 256).

The trap which causes such failures is, in a sense, man himself. Ponge demands that there should never be reference to man in "eidetic" poems (*M*, 255). By this, he does not really mean that all involvement of a human being in a work of art should cease— clearly an impossibility, despite Ponge's predilection for a non-human subject matter—but that anthropocentric views of the nonhuman world are misleading, inadequate, even perhaps insulting. The disservice these views do to things is well demonstrated by certain practices in the linguistic "manège," notably the use of figures of speech. Ponge takes exception to the phrase "a heart of stone" (*M*, 255). In speaking this way, man has insulted stone by stealing it for his own purposes, drastically narrowing its definition as a consequence. A stone is hard, Ponge does not deny it— although he might have conceded that "hard" is anthropocentric, given that the stone does not know itself to be hard—but it is other things too. If the observer, the writer, manages to bring out other qualities of stone (or rather, more accurately, if he allows the stone to express its other qualities, which is closer to Ponge's meaning), then that person has extricated himself from the "manège." It is possible, says Ponge, that the pieces of writing which result when his program of recommendations is followed may not be what are conventionally recognized as poems. This is merely bad luck for the reader; it is of no real importance.

He then goes on to make a statement which at first glance would have us believe that he does not consider himself a poet (a contention which he puts forward with greater conviction in *Méthodes* [40]). He says that he scorns poems, but instead accepts that he creates "poésies," by which he must mean texts which conform to the aesthetic laws of poetry without necessarily respecting the conventions of form. In fact, he implies that formal considerations are misguided, and lead back to the "manège": "Il ne s'agit pas d'arranger les choses....Il faut que les choses vous dérangent" ("It is not a matter of ordering things....It is necessary that things should disturb you," *M*, 251).

Ponge ends his discussion of this issue in these particular pages by throwing in the judgment, which has been echoed by various critics, that his type of language and poetry reflects a scientific as much as a poetic spirit. The message is clear that the old modes of poetic rhetoric are dead for him, and that he is trying to invent a new one. Rules, obstacles, difficulties must not be allowed to form part of that rhetoric and to seduce the poet into forgetting what exactly it was that he had to say, for his unswerving task is to bring into the open the truth of that which he is contemplating (*P*, 255). One of Ponge's several aphoristic statements neatly encapsulates his aesthetic principle of supplying a language which tries to get the measure of things as they disclose themselves: "Relever le défi des choses au langage" ("Take up the challenge issued to language by things," *T*, 291).

Ponge's acute awareness of the nature and function (also the malfunction) of language, his wish to be entirely radical in his handling of it, is further demonstrated in his notion of "writing against words" ("contre le mot" or "contre la parole"), the last of Ponge's attitudes of resistance to be considered here. Three quotations seem particularly pertinent: "Quant aux qualités de l'objet qui ne dépendent pas tant de son nom que de tout autre chose, ma tentative d'expression de ces qualités doit se produire plutôt *contre le mot* qui les offusquerait, qui tendrait à les annihiler..." ("As for the qualities of the object which do not depend so much on their name as on any other thing, my attempt at expressing these qualities must be made *against the word* which might obscure it, or lead to its annihilation...," *M*, 35). This counterthrust is aimed at all acts of language, except presumably those in which the object coincides exactly with its name (this must be an allusion to "adéquation"). In another book, Ponge writes: "Il faut d'abord parler, et à ce moment peu importe, dire n'importe quoi. Comme un départ au pied dans le jeu de rugby: foncer à travers les paroles, malgré les paroles, les entraîner avec soi, les bousculant, les défigurant" ("One must first speak, and at that point it does not matter, one should say anything at all. Like the kickoff in a rugby football game: one must crash through words, in spite of words, drag them along with one, knocking them about, disfiguring them," *T*, 216).

The extreme reverence for language which Ponge seems to maintain almost as an article of faith elsewhere has apparently been replaced by brutality. Is this merely coarse-minded and lazy? Ponge adopts very much the same position in another part of *Proêmes*, from which the last extract was taken: "*Une seule issue: parler contre les paroles. Les entraîner avec soi dans la honte où elles nous conduisent de telle sorte qu'elles s'y défigurent*" ("*Only one way out: speak against words. Drag them with oneself into the shame where they are leading us, so that they become disfigured,*" *T*, 186). The answer seems to be that Ponge is waging a crusader's war against an insidious and widespread evil, and that to be effective he has to attack ruthlessly, perhaps indiscriminately. The resultant disfiguration will have the hygienic properties of an eidetic cleansing. In fact, Ponge is as close as ever to his concept of a careful and precise language in the service of objects. There is certainly other evidence that he is concerned, in his "speaking against words," with bad linguistic practices of the sort already mentioned. He is neither coarse nor lazy, but determined rather to hack away at the choking growth of unnecessary language. This is not a new feature.

What is new in the notion of "writing against words" is the more subtle realization that language is resistant to man, and that by virtue of that very resistance the writer can make something more solid than if there were no opposition. To show what he means by the resistance of language, and what a constructive concept it is, Ponge makes an analogy with the wind in the trees (*M*, 249). The tree "speaks" out aloud, expresses itself, only when the wind activates it. Everything then indicates an indissoluble bond between wind and tree, a bond so close that it is invidious to attempt to distinguish between the two in terms of cause and effect, or active and passive participants. Ponge asks if it is the wind or the tree which has taken the decision to speak. What does the forest express when it speaks? Is the sound an expression of resistance to the wind, a "speaking against the wind," or is it on the contrary an approval of it? Welcome or rebuff? It could equally be said that the forest is taking responsibility for the movement of the wind, singing and dancing in captivating unison with it. On the other hand, it might be claimed that it is arguing with the wind, suffering and crying. The permanent paradox is that both the wind and the trees are simultaneously the instrument and the instrumentalist.

Ponge's message is that the same relationship exists between man and language. Like the wind, man can express nothing if he does not come up against a constraint, which would give him a voice. The constraint is language. His self-expression would be doomed to remain in the realm of the virtual. But when he finds language—and Ponge means the pure type of language which is his constant preoccupation—then there ensues his necessary and inevitable self-expression, comparable to the wind in the trees. Man and language become continuous; resistance and confrontation are literally creative.

In *Pour un Malherbe* (254), Ponge invokes but paradoxically damns Valéry's and the scholar René Fromilhague's versions of the same theme. These two hold that the creative mind needs to lean on something, to create resistances. It finds resistances in conventions of all sorts; the inherent difficulty of creating art actually produces ideas. (It is this claim which angers Ponge, and reaffirms him in his "anti-ideas" position). For Valéry, the rules of prosody are the necessary barrier reefs on which the waves of vague thinking, intentions, and impulses break, and the resultant crash causes new and unexpected figures to be formed. For all his dislike of Valéry, Ponge seems to be close to him in this matter of resistances.

Before leaving this question, it is worth noting that there is an echo, albeit a distant one, of the surrealists' endeavor with language, "la subversion surréaliste," as Sollers puts it.[7] Ponge was linked with surrealists, of course, around 1929 and 1930, and it could be argued that the will to break away from these linguistic habits which veil reality in all its dazzling immediacy—surrealism is a matter of knowing this brilliance which is available in the here-and-now, if only we could learn to see it—is what Ponge and the surrealists have in common. However, here they part company, for the surrealists headed into the extravagance and potential anarchy of automatic writing, with its insistence on disgorging all the chaotic contents of the subconscious and unconscious mind, an aesthetic clearly in total contrast with Ponge's carefully controlled coaxing out of the essences of things.

II   *A New Rhetoric*

After this survey of the sorts of language to which Ponge is opposed, the next task is to examine what he seeks to put in their place. In the foregoing section of this chapter, it will have become clear that Ponge stands in a particular, even idiosyncratic, relationship with objects, as well as with language. The two are, of course, indissolubly bound to each other, but it might be helpful to look first at some of Ponge's attitudes to and pronouncements about the material world.

First and foremost, the material world exists. This trite observation emerges time and again in Ponge's work as a matter of the greatest moment, and a lot of what he says is rooted in his conviction that too many artists of every sort lose this miraculous fact from sight. The sheer existence, the weighty "there-ness" of the nonhuman world is an overwhelming fact that cannot and must not be disguised by anyone, especially not by the creative artist who wants to "arrange" matters to suit his own convenience. Ponge's awareness of this insistent presence of the world is not unlike Roquentin's in Sartre's *La Nausée*. Both Ponge and Roquentin are awakened, Ponge in a quiet way, from his earliest age, Roquentin in a dramatic and nauseating illumination, to the momentous, permanently unsettling truth that the world exists autonomously, independently of the containing exercises men do upon it. In very distinct ways, Ponge and Roquentin realize that overcomplacent linguistic categories fail to tame the natural world; it continues to be wild and elusive. This blinding intuition of the irreducibility of the world makes Roquentin sick, perhaps pathologically so. Ponge, on the other hand, gives various indications that this same knowledge is a source of awe—there is on occasion a quasi-mystical tone about his celebration of things—and an impetus to validate himself both as a writer and as a human being by devoting his creative energies to the service of the material world. What Ponge has done, in the phrase Sartre used when writing about *Le Parti pris des choses*,[8] is to understand that "L'être préexiste au connaître" ("being preexists knowing").

The mention at this point of Ponge's first major book, *Le Parti pris des choses*, is appropriate. The very title is an important pointer, and not free of ambiguities. It can mean, and is usually taken this way, "to take the side of things". That is, the bias ("parti pris") is attributed to man, who maintains it in favor of things. But this leaves out the possibility of exactly the opposite meaning, "the side things take." By extension, this second meaning may involve the notion of the set purpose, the obstinacy of things, their refusal to allow easy access to man. They are thus impenetrable, hermetically apart in the privacy of their "en-soi." Furthermore, this meaning might imply that things have a stubborn will to express themselves, and this suggests the title of another of Ponge's books, *La Rage de l'expression*. Beth Archer has dealt with these possibilities, including the more subtle one that "parti pris" implies an arbitrary and partial quality, a prejudice perhaps, in the expression which men give to the world through their words and their literature.[9] Sartre gives further paraphrases of the title, which seem less self-evident.[10] He proposes three readings: (1) to take the side of things against man, (2) to think in terms of, to accept, the existence of things over and above the idealism which reduces the world to its representations, its images and (3) to see things exclusively in terms of an *a priori* aesthetic.

Yet another, but seemingly unlikely, reading is proposed by Sollers,[11] who opts not only for the acceptable "prejudice in favor of things," but also for "resigned to things." However, this last suggestion would run counter to the tone of celebration in Ponge when he deals with the material world. It is interesting to note that Ponge originally had another title ready for *Le Parti pris des choses*, which was *L'Approbation de la Nature* (*P*, 186). It is more crude than the preferred title, but it does give a hint that the bias is man's and not nature's—unless, which seems dubious, given normal usage, nature's approbation of something else is being suggested. Perhaps Ponge rejected this title because it too readily excluded the meaning of "nature as subject," not merely as object.

A well-known incident brought together the two strands. At the end of a lecture, given in Brussels in January 1947, Ponge bent forward to kiss the table at which he was sitting: "Chère table, adieu! (Voyez-vous, si je l'aime, c'est que rien en elle ne permet de croire qu'elle se prenne pour un piano)" ("Dear table, goodbye! [You see, if I love it, it is because nothing about it allows it to be taken for a piano]," *M*, 262). Ponge's sentimental "parti pris" for objects is plain to see, while his parenthetical explanation shows that the table has the virtue of being nothing except itself, of remaining irreducible.

Ponge's attitude to objects (and, it could be argued, to language as well) has more than a suspicion of mysticism about it. This is very apparent when he writes about the privileged moment of the object's achievement of self-expression: "le moment de la vérité, c'est lorsque la vérité *jouit*....C'est le moment où l'objet jubile, si je puis dire, sort de lui-même ses qualités...." ("the moment of truth is when truth takes pleasure....It is the moment when the object exults, so to speak, produces from within itself its qualities...," *M*, 257). The same mystical tone is felt in those seminal texts contained in *Le Parti pris des choses* and *Proêmes*, for example, in "Ressources naïves" and "Introduction au galet," as well as in some from his other works, notably "A la rêveuse matière" which begins:

"Probablement tout et tous—et nous-mêmes—ne sommes-nous que des rêves immédiats de la divine Matière...("Probably all things and all people—including ourself—are only immediate dreams of divine Matter...," *N*, 177). Ponge goes on a few lines later: "Et ainsi, en un sens, pourrait-on dire que la nature entière, y compris les hommes, n'est qu'une écriture; mais une écriture d'un certain genre; une écriture *non-significative*, du fait qu'elle ne se réfère à aucun système de signification..." ("And so, in a sense, one could say that the whole of nature, men included, is nothing other than something written; but of a certain kind; *non-significant* writing, because it does not refer to any signifying system..."). Despite this adherence to the principle of nature's agrammaticality, Ponge surely reveals a kind of secular mysticism in his wish to allow the world to speak, to decipher itself.

In the long, theoretical "Introduction au galet" (*T*, 196-202), Ponge has some important lines about the place of things: "à propos, de n'importe quoi seulement tout n'est pas dit, mais à peu près tout reste à dire" ("about anything at all, not only has everything not been said, but just about everything remains to be said"); "Il suffit...de fixer son attention sur le premier objet venu: on s'apercevra aussitôt que personne ne l'a jamais observé, et qu'à son propos les choses les plus élémentaires restent à dire" ("It is enough...to fix one's attention on the first object encountered: one will immediately realize that no one has ever observed it, and that the most elementary things remain to be said about it"); "Tout le secret du bonheur du contemplateur est dans son refus de considérer *comme un mal* l'envahissement de sa personnalité par les choses" ("The whole secret of the beholder's happiness lies in his refusal to consider it *an evil thing* to have his personality invaded by things"); and finally, in a possible reference to Lucretius: "je voudrais écrire une sorte de *De natura rerum*" ("I would like to write a kind of *On the nature of things*").

However, Ponge's perhaps most telling piece on his cult of objects is contained in his essay "La Pratique de la littérature." At the relevant point in this essay, he is setting out to explain what it is that he means by "parti pris des choses" (*M*, 268-72). In what may seem a prose equivalent of Nerval's "Vers dorés," Ponge writes:

Nous sommes des hommes, des femmes, vous m'écoutez, je parle. Mais ça continue dehors. Tout fonctionne. La terre, le système, il faut se mettre dans cette idée, tout fonctionne, tout marche, ça passe, ça tourne, et non seulement les herbes poussent, très lentement mais très sûrement, les pierres attendent d'éclater ou devenir du sable. Ici, les objets vivent aussi. Il y en a partout, nous sommes environnés de témoins muets, muets, tandis que nous....En tout cas, cette réalité non seulement du fonctionnement (ce serait presque rassurant), mais de l'existence probablement aussi dramatique que la nôtre, des moindres objets,—vous comprenez—, qui s'en occupe? Tous les livres de la bibliothèque universelle depuis des siècles traitent de l'homme, de la femme, des rapports entre les hommes et les femmes....Souhaitons donc, une fois seulement, quelque chose de profondément respectueux, simplement un peu d'attention, de pitié peut-être ou de sympathie, pour ces rangs, ces rangées de choses muettes qui ne peuvent pas s'exprimer, sinon par des poses, des façons d'être, des formes auxquelles elles sont contraintes, qui sont leur damnation comme nous avons la nôtre.

We are men, women, you listen to me, I speak. But outside, things are continuing. All is functioning. The earth, the system, we must get used to the idea, all is functioning, all is working, it goes on, it turns, and not only do plants grow, very slowly but very surely, but stones wait to split, or to turn into sand. Here, objects live as well. They are all around, we are surrounded by silent, silent witnesses, while we....Anyway this reality not only of this functioning system (this would be almost reassuring), but of the existence, probably as dramatic as our own, of the smallest objects—you understand—who bother themselves with it? All the books in the universal library for several centuries have dealt with men and women, with relationships between men and women....Let us hope, just once, for something profoundly respectful, simply a little attention, pity perhaps or sympathy for these rows, these lines of silent things which cannot express themselves except by poses, by their ways of being, by the forms which constrain them, which are their curse, as we have ours.

Interestingly, Ponge goes on, a page or two later, to recognize that people might see him as a mystic: "Vous me direz: 'votre attitude envers les choses est mystique'" ("You will say to me: 'Your attitude toward things is mystical'"). No, Ponge replies, it is not; rather, it is a question of saying honestly, authentically, all that there is to say about an object. This is the only tenable position for the poet; it is what Ponge calls in the same essay a sensitivity to things as things. To round off his argument, he refers to La Fontaine's pieces about the "lion grown old," or the "sick lion," or the "lion and the stork." Ponge's aim (and this distinction is crucial) is to write about "the lion," "the horse." His aim is to be definitive and complete, even though this will involve epithetic and approximative stages on the way.

It might be added that Ponge's choice of objects about which to write—those objects which, in another semimystical passage, he calls his "pretext," a pun on "pretext/pre-text" (*M*, 12-13)—is eclectic. As he says in the same passage: "*la variété des choses est en réalité ce qui me construit*" ("*the variety of things is what in reality constructs me*"). Ponge can range from texts about mud, pebbles, cigarettes, packing-crates, to others about snails, butterflies, gymnasts, young mothers. In all, the same process of reification is at work, whether the subject (or object) of the text is human, animate, vegetable, or mineral. The subject is made object.

Some critics, notably Sartre and Jean-Pierre Richard, have discerned patterns in Ponge's choice of suitable matter. Sartre has pointed to a taste for the solid[12] while Richard claims that he finds a predilection for what he calls punctual, insular, discontinuous things, such as a drop of water, a crumb, a snail, a pebble, a shrimp. Furthermore, this kind of discrete object is often marked by its open, active, and flourishing qualities.[13] Given the wealth of things and objects Ponge has written about, and their disparity, Sartre's and Richard's points are telling. One quotation from Ponge himself demonstrates the passage from the formless to the well-defined: "Mais le monde est peuplé d'objets. Sur ses rivages, leur foule infinie, leur collection nous apparaît, certes, plutôt indistincte et floue....Pourtant cela suffit à nous rassurer. Car, nous l'éprouvons aussi, chacun d'eux à notre gré, tour à tour, peut devenir notre point d'amarrage, la borne où nous appuyer....Il suffit qu'il fasse le poids" ("But the world is inhabited by objects. On its shores, the unending crowd of them, the collection of them seem to us, certainly, rather indistinct and blurred....Yet that is enough to reassure us. For, something we experience as well, each of them, to our liking, by turns, can become our mooring point, the bollard on which we can lean....It is enough that they should be up to it," *N*, 147). Viscosity becomes solidity as men realize their relationship of interdependence with the material world.

This survey of Ponge's pronouncements on the material world reveals, apart from a quasi-religious awe of the objects, a kind of Pythagorean belief that the inanimate is intelligent, but is also permanently frustrated in the desire it may have to express itself. Man must therefore intervene. So, when Ponge apparently considers objects as discrete entities, he cannot disguise the reality and the necessity of a human involvement.

A. *Language and Objects*

Consideration of objects as objects leads Ponge to somewhat guilty conclusions about man's responsibility to them. The next aspect of his poetics to discuss, therefore, is his attitude toward language as it relates man to the material world. A useful introduction to such a discussion is the text taking as its title a quotation from Braque, "l'objet c'est la poétique" (*N*, 143). The text begins: "Le rapport de l'homme à l'objet n'est du tout seulement de possession ou d'usage. Non, ce serait trop simple. C'est bien pire.... Les objets sont en dehors de l'âme, bien sûr; pourtant, ils sont aussi notre plomb dans la tête" ("The relationship of man to object is not at all just one of possession or of usage. No, that would be too simple. It's a lot worse.... Objects are outside our souls, of course; and yet, they are also the weighty matter which fills our heads").

Sounding like a philosopher, Ponge is making the transition from pure materialism (a philosophical position which might seem inevitable on those occasions when he speaks like a physicist) to phenomenology, to an acceptance that objects are as they appear in consciousness, and, more particularly for this poet, as they appear in linguistic thought. Ponge lends support to phenomenology's adherence to intentionality when he adds, with epigrammatic terseness: "Notre âme est transitive." That is, consciousness needs an object; "consciousness" is "consciousness of." Ponge reconciles the insistent needs of objects and of human beings; the latter need the former as complements of their consciousness, the former need the latter as agents who will effect their expression. The point of interest in this idea is that Ponge considers it vital that things, objects, should be described from their own point of view, and not from man's. In short, he is reaffirming his hostility to anthropocentric thought and art (see *T*, 503). He can be quite eloquent in advancing the cause of objects: "Il reconnaîtra aussitôt l'importance de chaque chose, et la muette supplication, les muettes instances qu'elles font qu'on les parle, à leur valeur, et pour elles-mêmes,—en dehors de leur valeur habituelle de signification,—sans choix et pourtant avec mesure, mais quelle mesure: la leur propre" ("He [man] will immediately admit the importance of each thing, and the silent supplication, the silent entreaties they make that we should utter them, on their merits and for their own sakes—leaving aside what is normally held to be their significance—without imposing our choices, and yet with regard to proportion, but what proportion: their very own," *T,* 137). A crucial part of this quotation is the grammatically surprising "les muettes instances qu'elles font qu'on les parle," where the more predictable indirect object pronoun ("leur") has given way to the direct ("les"), changing the meaning from "to speak about" to "to speak a thing," in other words, "to allow the thing to have a voice." This is typical of Ponge's grammatical usage in the service of his precise meaning. Elsewhere, he writes: "O ressources infinies de l'épaisseur des choses, *rendues* par les ressources infinies de l'épaisseur sémantique des mots!" ("O infinite resources of the density of things, *rendered* by the infinite resources of the semantic density of words!" *T,* 200). Ponge himself has italicized the past participle "*rendues,*" making it quite clear that his meaning is "rendered," or perhaps "delivered," "brought out"; the meaning he does not intend is "translated" or "symbolized," or even "denoted."

The concept of language as a system of symbols, specially constructed as convenient shorthand to indicate the world, is rejected by Ponge. Language does not stand in such a secondary position. His contempt for the hollow, anthropocentric use of language and his constant attempt to reinstate objects led Ponge to the position in respect of objects which has been discussed in the foregoing paragraphs. There emerges also from the same factors a comparable position in respect of language. The reinstatement of objects and that of a valid language go hand in hand, and are both characterized by a tendency to reification.

B. *Language as Substance and Object*

Some remarks about language as substance are now appropriate. In a way which has some unlikely echoes of the English romantic poet Coleridge ("I would endeavour to destroy the old antithesis of Words and Things: elevating, as it were Words into Things and living Things too"),[14] Ponge has made a number of statements about the substantiality of language, which he sees as both part of man and at the same time distinct from him. To illustrate this, he has drawn an analogy between, on the one hand, man and language, and on the other, certain shelled animals and what he terms their "secretion." The five texts which more than others exemplify this concept are "Le mollusque," "Escargots," and "Notes pour un coquillage," all in *Le Parti pris des choses*, and "Des raisons d'écrire" and "Raisons de vivre heureux," both in *Proêmes*. In "Notes pour un coquillage," Ponge lists those creative artists—Bach, Rameau, Horace, Malherbe, Mallarmé—whom he admires for their sense of proportion, and then he adds that of these he most admires the writers because "leur monument est fait de la véritable sécrétion commune du mollusque homme, de la chose la plus proportionnée et conditionnée à son corps, et cependant la plus différente de sa forme que l'on puisse concevoir: je veux dire LA PAROLE" ("their monument is made of the truly universal secretion of the mollusc Man, of the thing most proportionate and conditioned to his body, and yet as different from his form as can be conceived: I mean THE WORD," *T*, 86).

The purpose of the analogy is to suggest that language ("parole" may mean "spoken word" or "speech," but Ponge wants it to bring together all the forms of expression inherent in language) is a substance as well as a quality, and that it is at the same time an integral part of man and something which he secretes *out* of himself. Likewise, the shells of crustaceans and molluscs are significant for Ponge in that they are external to the animal (they are its secretion), and yet the animal without its shell must necessarily cease to exist. The poem "Escargots" takes the form of a fable-meditation on the snail. It is a remarkable piece, a sustained examination of, and reflection on, the properties of the snail, and as it progresses to its climax, it becomes apparent that its moral, giving it its fablelike tone, concerns the link which Ponge establishes between the snail's and man's form of secretion. The snail, first, secretes its silver trail of slime as it progresses majestically along the ground to which it seems to be stuck. If this were its only expression (for Ponge certainly sees it as the expression of the snail's anger and of its pride), then the snail would indeed be ephemeral, even during its own lifetime. But it has its shell, and this constitutes the "moral," the "lesson" which it can give. For, unlike those (that is, human beings) who have not taken the trouble to build a solid structure of their self-expression, and who have instead expressed themselves only through the ephemera of subjective and vanishing traces, the snail has got its monument, its work of art which will outlast the animal inside it—the shell. Furthermore, this work of art is perfect in that it is proportioned, measured exactly to the needs of snails: "Rien d'extérieur à eux, à leur nécessité, à leur besoin n'est leur oeuvre" ("Nothing which is exterior to them, to their necessity, to their need, is their work," *T*, 61). For this reason, Ponge calls snails saints; they make of their lives a work of art. Also, their secretion itself is produced in such a way as to take on a definite form; it is made solid substance.

Now Ponge can finish his fable by drawing the moral conclusions for man. Snails are saints inasmuch as they are in perfect accord with their nature, which they obey unquestioningly. Man must aim to do the same, know himself first and foremost, know his vices, be in tune with them, and be in proportion with his dimensions. How is he to do this? By the exercise of language: "quelle est la notion propre de l'homme: la parole et la morale. L'humanisme" ("what is the notion specific to man: the word and morals. Humanism"). Although the implications of human presence will have to be looked at elsewhere in this book, Ponge's message here is that language should be man's properly formed shell, and that it is his ethical imperative to arrive at it.

In "Le mollusque" (*T*, 55-56), Ponge pursues his crustacean analogy when he reveals a similarity between the interdependence of flesh and shell in a mollusc, and that of man and language. The flesh is in itself formless, and depends wholly on the shell for contour. There is no way of taking the flesh out alive. Similarly, says Ponge, "La moindre cellule du corps de l'homme tient ainsi, et avec cette force, à la parole,—et réciproquement" ("The least cell of man's body depends on the word—and vice versa"). The use of "tenir" is subtle; Ponge doubtless intends it to have its meaning of "to insist on," "to value," as well as "to hold." The biological, in a sense the behavioristic, view of language could hardly be put more strongly. Ponge concludes his text on another moral, cautionary note. Sometimes, when the flesh inside the shell has died, its place is taken, the tomb is violated, by the hermit crab. It is a well-wrought irony with which to finish his text, and it may be assumed that Ponge is aiming his irony at man's various "violations" of authentic language.

In at least one text, Ponge expresses his notion of "language as secretion" by means of an analogy not connected with shelled animals, but which is still drawn from the natural world. In fact, he uses one of his favorite analogies, men compared to trees, when, in "Raisons de vivre heureux," he concludes his meditation on how man may live happily with this paragraph about the way in which the artist creates and releases works appropriate to each stage of his development: "Le sujet, le poème de chacune de ces périodes correspondant évidemment à l'essentiel de l'homme à chacun de ses âges; comme les successives écorces d'un arbre, se détachant par l'effort naturel de l'arbre à chaque époque" ("The subject, the poem of each of these periods obviously corresponding to what is essential in man at each of his ages; like the successive barks of a tree, shed by the natural effort of the tree at each appropriate time," *T*, 190). Ponge's narrowing of the scope of his notion of "secretion" from all languages to the particular practices of the writer will serve as an introduction to his equally important view that language, especially as used in poetry, is an object.

Despite the evidence set out in the last paragraph, Ponge tends to refuse, in theory at least, analogical language. Its obvious pitfall for him is that it predicates a permanent separateness of the two terms of a comparison, and perpetuates the symbolists' error which was to dig a trench between thing and word.[15] In opposition to the analogical mode, Ponge puts forward the program of a poetic language ("écriture") turned into object through its self-referring activity: "La production de son propre signe devenant ainsi la condition de l'accomplissement de quoi que ce soit....c'est bien ainsi qu'il faut concevoir l'écriture: non comme la transcription, selon un code conventionnel, de quelque idée (extérieure ou antérieure) ..." ("The production of its own sign thus becoming the condition of the accomplishment of anything whatsoever...it is in this way that one must conceive of writing: not as the transcription, according to the conventions of a code, of some idea [exterior or anterior]...")[16]

Ponge completes his argument by drawing on what he sees as the essential characteristic of orgasm. The type of language he wants will be "comme l'orgasme d'une [*sic*] être, ou disons d'une structure, déjà conventionnelle par elle-même, bien entendu—mais qui doit, pour s'accomplir, se donner, avec jubilation, comme telle: en un mot, se signifier elle-même" ("Like the orgasm of a being, or let us say of a structure, already conventional through its existence, of course— but which, in order to fulfill itself, must give itself, with jubilation, as such: in a word, it must signify itself"). "Jubilation" is an idea which quite frequently occurs in Ponge's work, and conveys the particular joy, or celebration, of acting in perfect harmony with the self, of being totally accurate in self-expression. Orgasm, claims Ponge, is a powerful example of a joyful experience which obliterates all considerations outside itself.

The final paragraph of *Le Savon*, a very long text devoted to the minute examination of soap from all conceivable angles, but more, a *construction* of a poem-object to match the material substance, has the effect of releasing the completed text so that it may take its place, and its chance, in the world of time and space: "Voilà donc ce livre bouclé; notre toupie lancée; notre SAVON en orbite.... (Et tous les *étages* ou chapitres successifs mis à feu pour sa lancée peuvent bien, déjà, être retombés dans l'*atmosphere*, lieu commun de l'oubli, comme il fut celui du projet.)...Son sort ne dépend plus que de la nature matérielle dont ces signes et leur support font partie" ("So there's this book all wrapped up; our spinning-top set in motion; our SOAP in orbit....[And all the *stages* or successive chapters, ignited for its launch may well have already fallen back into the *atmosphere*, the common place of oblivion, as it was that of the project.]...Its fate now depends only on material nature of which these signs and their supports are a part," *S*, 128). In a piece which depends quite manifestly on the rhetoric of analogical language, Ponge launches his poem-object like a craft to be buffeted in the air, and to run the risks of accident, even disintegration; or it may survive.

Not surprisingly, the majority of Ponge's pronouncements on language as substance and object are to be found in *Méthodes*; there are others in *Pour un Malherbe*, while *Le Parti pris des choses* contains at least one interesting text in this respect. First, in *Méthodes*, he speaks of the autonomy and the personality of words: "Aucun mot n'est employé qui ne soit considéré aussitôt comme une personne" ("No word is used which is not immediately considered as a person," *M*, 32). Ponge amplifies a few lines later: "Lorsque j'admets un mot à la sortie, lorsque je fais sortir un mot, aussitôt je dois le traiter non comme un élément quelconque, un bout de bois, un fragment de puzzle, mais comme un pion ou une figure, une personne à trois dimensions, etc....et je ne peux en jouer exactement à ma guise" ("When I allow a word to leave, when I make a word go out, I must immediately treat it not just as some element or other, a piece of wood, a fragment of a puzzle, but as a pawn or a figure, a three-dimensional person etc....and I can't play around with it as I please," *M*, 33). Ponge is not so much denying the status of language as object when he refuses to look at words as pieces of wood or fragments of a puzzle—a denial which would contradict his normal position—as accepting it in order to go beyond and to focus on the living condition of words which, as figures and people, have their own will and exigencies. They make impositions on those who would use them. They are there, presences, three-dimensional and concrete.

Ponge says more about these last aspects in another part of *Méthodes.* In "La Pratique de la littérature" he states that, as well as a sensitivity to the exterior world, the writer must have "une autre sensibilité à un autre monde, entièrement concret également, bizarrement concret, mais concret, qui est le langage, les mots" ("another sensitivity to another world, also entirely concrete, strangely concrete, but concrete, which is language, words," *M*, 271). Then, two pages later, he picks up this idea: "Les mots, c'est bizarrement concret, parce que, si vous pensez...en même temps ils ont, mettons deux dimensions, pour l'oeil et pour l'oreille, et peut-être la troisième c'est quelque chose comme leur signification" ("Words are strangely concrete, because, when you think about it...they have at the same time, let's say, two dimensions, for the eye and for the ear, and perhaps the third is something like their significance," *M*, 272-73). And a page later, Ponge repeats this almost word for word, but adds that "le mot est un objet à trois dimensions, donc un objet vraiment" ("the word is a three-dimensional object, therefore truly an object," *M*, 274).

Here and there in *Pour un Malherbe*, Ponge scatters remarks on the same subject. He writes of the precise and necessary mutual reflection of objects and language (*P*, 73-74), and in a later passage he declares a taste for those texts which have the solidity and fixity of stone. For a text to be "valid," he says, it must be of the sort which can be inscribed in stone. This is the only sort which he himself can sign, or countersign, with honesty. Yet, the authentic texts of this kind are those which, paradoxically, cannot be signed; those which take their place among nature's objects, in the open air, in the sun, the rain, the wind. Hence his taste for inscriptions, for the Roman inscriptions at Nîmes (*P*, 186).

In the next paragraph, Ponge brings in the philosophy of the Stoics, more particularly as it relates to science: "En somme, j'approuve la Nature..., exactement par stoïcisme..." ("In short, *I approve of Nature...*, precisely through stoicism..."). This is an idea which does not come up often in Ponge's work, but when it does, it has considerable pertinence. In a text already looked at in some of its aspects, "Escargots," Ponge calls the snail "stoical," because it stays put, it is in no hurry to move or to flee (*T,* 59). Stoicism is perhaps being used with its popular connotation of facing silently and uncomplainingly all kinds of fortune; but there may also be an allusion to Stoic physics, especially if one looks at another reference to Stoicism, this one in *Méthodes* (122). In a somewhat dense paragraph, Ponge discusses a statement once made by Charlie Chaplin—"I never taste rhum [*sic*]"—in terms of what he sees as Chaplin's adherence to the principle of "Le parti pris des choses." The point, conceivably, is that the drinker, held at a distance by the stubbornness, the apartness of the thing called rum, cannot make contact with it; he may drink it, but he cannot absorb it as part of himself.

After mentioning Epicureanism (presumably a passing allusion to its theory of knowledge based on sensations), Ponge finishes the paragraph with a reference to the fact that Stoicism both does and does not resemble Epicureanism. In this context, the likely explanation as to why Ponge lets these names drop is that, in Stoic physics, the reason for the existence of things is not that they should attain a goal external to them, but rather that they may act, live out their lives in accordance with how they are. The purpose of a stone or a snail lies within the stone and the snail; their purpose is to be what they are. Such a philosophy would clearly have an appeal for a man such as Ponge; its materialism, acting against anthropocentric attitudes, makes silent heroes out of objects. What is more, it might well be that the Stoics' ideas about the soul and spirit of the material world would have some appeal for Ponge, given the mystical tendencies of his thinking about objects.

So, objects must be revealed in their fulness, their granitic solidity. In his poetics, Ponge goes to some lengths to convey to his readers the important facts of the apartness and of the sheer presence of objects. He wants to do the same for language, and consideration of this matter can be appropriately concluded by quoting the somewhat grandiloquent final paragraph of "La promenade dans nos serres": "O traces humaines à bout de bras, ô sons originaux, monuments de l'enfance de l'art, quasi imperceptibles modifications physiques, CARACTÈRES, objets mystérieux perceptibles par deux sens seulement et cependant plus réels, plus sympathiques que signes,—je veux vous rapprocher de la substance et vous éloigner de la qualité. Je veux vous faire aimer pour vous-mêmes plutôt que pour votre signification. Enfin vous élever à une condition plus noble que celle de simples désignations" ("O human traces at the end of the arm, o original sounds, monuments of art's infancy, almost imperceptible physical modifications, LETTERS, mysterious objects perceptible only by two senses and yet more real, more engaging than signs—I want to get you closer to substance and further from quality. I want you to be loved for yourselves rather than for your significance. In short, to elevate you to a nobler condition than that of simple designations," *T*, 146).

Some critics have contributed worthwhile comments on Ponge's language-object assimilation. Jean Thibaudeau makes the obvious point that Ponge operates on the basis that there is a fundamental distinction between expression and communication,[17] and later remarks that the ideal function of a writer such as Ponge would be to place his text at the point where the world and language intersect. Werner Wider remarks that if language is intended to be equal to its object, then it must itself be an object in the sense that it must be as "inexplicable" as an object.[18] Finally, and most interestingly, Sartre sees a parallel between the series of phrases and sentences in Ponge and the solids created in their paintings by Braque and Gris.[19] In these paintings, the viewer is obliged to do the work himself of establishing links and correspondences between the solids, of building them into many different unities, so as to arrive at a single picture; and yet, he is constantly sent back, by the firmness of contour, the self-centeredness of each solid, from the continuous to the discontinuous. The mandolin, the water jug, favored objects of these painters, remain impenetrable.

C. *"Objeu," "Objoie," "En Abîme"*

Ponge calls the method used to bring about the successful "self-assertion" of objects by a portmanteau word, "objeu," and the human emotional response to this by another, "objoie." The "objeu" (compounded of "objet" and "jeu"), says Ponge, is the method "où l'objet de notre émotion placé d'abord en abîme, l'épaisseur vertigineuse et l'absurdité du langage, considérées seules, sont manipulées de telle façon que, par la multiplication intérieure des rapports, les liaisons formées au niveau des racines et les significations bouclées à double tour, soit créé ce fonctionnement qui seul peut rendre compte de la profondeur substantielle, de la variété et de la rigoureuse harmonie du monde" ("by which the object of our emotion placed first of all at the abyss of the escutcheon, the vertiginous thickness and the absurdity of language, considered in isolation, are manipulated in such a way that, through the internal multiplication of relationships, links having been formed at the level of the roots of words and meanings securely locked in, that functioning is created which alone can give an account of the substantial depth, of the variety and of the rigorous harmony of the world").[20] First of all, "en abîme" in all likelihood refers to the abyss, or the fess-point, of an escutcheon; the French phrase is here given its comparatively rare heraldic meaning of the "dead center" of a coat-of-arms.

This was brought into literature as a critical metaphor by the Gide of the *Journal* and the *Nourritures terrestres* to convey the concept of the simultaneous diversity and unity of a piece of writing. Gide's idea was that the whole of a work of art should be discernible in the parts, just as the parts are in the whole; and the individual parts should provide a sort of reciprocal enlightenment. In other words, a work of art, especially for Gide a piece of writing, right down to the individual sentence, should be composed of mirrors, creating a kaleidoscope of internal reflections, and adding up to a multifaceted but unified entity. This interpretation of the "en abîme" concept suits Ponge's text "Le soleil placé en abîme." The sun is at the epicenter, and just as it radiates light, so linguistically it opens up a wealth of dazzling possibilities. One definition of it reflects a second, which in turn mirrors a third, and so on. The concept of the fess-point goes a long way toward explaining why Ponge is so given to the technique of building up patterns of repeated phrases which are partial definitions, modifying the phrases slightly each time, imperceptibly adding to them, a procedure perhaps not unlike Péguy's.

To return to a broader consideration of the extract just quoted from "Le soleil placé en abîme," its meaning presumably comes down to this: after one has looked closely, and with an open mind, at an object in all its diversity, one then proceeds with a similar attitude to look at its equivalents in language, and finds that this language contains rich and deep-seated patterns and its own internal structures with can give the clue to the organization of the nonlinguistic world. In short, language is microcosmic where the world is macrocosmic. This is how Thibaudeau sees it too; the "objeu" groups together words according to its own laws of logic, it is an autonomous structure, no more nor less relative than reality itself.[21]

Ponge refers again to the "objeu" a few times in *Pour un Malherbe*. The theme which emerges from these references (as well as the one just quoted) is that of harmony. When language is working as it should, then the "lyre" being sounded gives out a proper resonance, and this is evidence of the "objeu" in action. "Cet instrument résonnera dès lors à tout propos, à propos de n'importe quoi. Il se définit aussi, en tant qu'instrument, par son extériorité par rapport à nous. Nous en jouons à volonté, ou le laissons dans le silence,—et voilà encore l'OBJEU" ("Then this instrument will sound at every turn, and on account of anything at all. Also it is defined, in its quality as an instrument, by its being external to us. We play it at will, or we let it remain silent—and here again is the OBJEU" *P*, 72). The close association between the "objeu" and a correct sound brings up the notion of "réson," a word invented by Ponge, and "raison" ("resonance" and "reason"), an association which must be examined later in this chapter.

The remainder of Ponge's references to the "objeu" are unhelpful, with the possible exception of one: "*L'Objeu* est ce que nous avons à promouvoir actuellement: 'primitivisme,' 'préciosité,' 'baroquisme,' 'classicisme' et 'romantisme' bouclés à double tour dans *chaque* texte" ("The *Objeu* is what we must promote at this moment: 'primitivism,' 'preciosity,' 'baroquism,' 'classicism,' and 'roman- ticism' firmly locked in in each text," *P*, 139). In its context, this means that language must contain all these aspects, it must be dense and laden with its own significance, before the developments and accidents of history impose their own brands from outside. So, Ponge claims that he can establish a link between his own historical period and that of Malherbe (one of the reasons, incidentally, for his having written *Pour un Malherbe*) through a similarity of a language whose authenticity transcends the accidental accretions of the intervening centuries: "Que l'Esprit, le Verbe, *précède* les institutions" ("May the Spirit, the Word, *precede* institutions") he writes on the same page.

The comments of three critics on this matter are rather more productive than what Ponge himself has to say. Neal Oxenhandler writes that the "objeu" is what Ponge calls "this playful interaction of human perceiver and the object, in which each reveals the nature of the other,"[22] while Richard also stresses the interdependence of perceiver and perceived when he speaks of Ponge's transformation of object into "objeu" in terms of something which has become porous, as it were, to the sensibility and to the mind.[23] Finally,

Albert Léonard sees the transformation of object into "objeu" as the result of the application of a rhetoric which is specific to each particular object.[24] The interesting feature is that these critics point to the necessary and obvious involvement of the writer in the elaboration of the "objeu," in contrast to the impression given in Ponge's own writing on the subject that he is trying to veil this truth behind some rather pompous phrases. The constant, basic, and simple question of poetics thrown up by Ponge's theories centers on how the objective world can speak for itself; when he talks of the "harmony of the world," he cannot disguise the fact that both this judgment and any attempt to render that harmony have to be anthropocentric. Fortunately, Ponge's creative work is generally more convincing than his theories.

Ponge has coined the word "objoie," and it is a kind of conceit to be taken together with the "objeu." He brings it in, though with no great clarity, as part of the fifth appendix to his long text *Le Savon*, under the heading of "Introduction à la morale de l'Objoie." In this appendix, he discusses the role of hands and the role of soap in the action of washing hands. The conclusion he seems to draw is that by using a piece of soap, an agent for cleanliness, one is made aware of the relationship, expressed by the word "with" in "washing with soap," between hands and the soap, and one reaches a full awareness of self (hands) as one realizes that the soap, so nearly assimilated to the hands in the rubbing action, is in fact distinct from them.

Figuratively, soap, on bringing this awareness, serves to cleanse the self of all its accretions, and it discloses identity. Personal identity in this pristine state then signifies only itself. It is able, says Ponge, to be made eternal in the "objoie," and finally paradise, turning around Sartre's aphorism, becomes others (*S*, 128). That is, a person defines himself in terms of all the things he is not; the consequent self-realization has the effect of turning a person into a sort of object. In this curious state of lucidity, where a person is both his own subject and object, the enclosed system of self-significance, like language in the "objeu," produces a sense of truth, and it is this, it seems, that is meant by "objoie" in the context of *Le Savon*. It is important that an agent external to the self is necessary—in this case, a piece of soap. The agent appears to be not so much dispensed with as incorporated into a constant dialectic whereby the "joie" elicited in the self by the agent then becomes directed in its turn at that agent, achieving the fuller "harmony of the world" mentioned in the last paragraph.

Oxenhandler says of "objoie" that it is "not ecstasy or delirium, but that simple pleasure in interaction with the things of this world that man can attain,"[25] and indeed one feels that the obscure paragraphs of *Le Savon*, which have been set out above, can be tidily reduced to this single clear statement. One last observation about the "objeu" and "objoie" is that both appear to be closely related to the activity of eidetic reduction in phenomenology; looking at objects, at the self made object, and at language made object, in the way prescribed by Ponge, surely involves the process of bracketing the world in order to perform a phenomenological inspection of it.

D. *"Raison"* and *"Réson"*

Mention has been made, in this discussion of the "objeu" and "objoie," of "raison" and "réson," and the implications of these two words must now be examined more fully, as they bear upon Ponge's ideas about authentic language, and lead in as well to the highly important issue of "adéquation." Ponge first deals with what he means by "raison" (leaving the introduction of "réson" until *Pour un Malherbe*) in one of the texts contained in *Proêmes*, and entitled "Des raisons d'écrire," in which the idea of "speaking against words" is also outlined. Ponge defines reason as "la nature *dans l'homme*" (*T*, 184), and the surrounding text reveals that this means the individual's ability to make all extraneous and superfluous noises and influences disappear in him, and to allow Nature, more powerful yet much quieter, to take possession of him.

Two texts later, Ponge deals more fully with "raison". In "Raisons de vivre heureux" (*T*, 188-90), he shows that what is involved is the refocusing of the mind on things. It is an openness of mind, alive to the true nature of the world, a welcome state which will inevitably lead to writing which, by concentrating intently on the external world, will seem to the unobservant to be merely description or pointless painting. But, as joy first came to Ponge through contemplation, it will return through painting, as this affords the joyful memory of the "objects of sensations." It is this activity which he calls "reasons for living." The precondition for success in this area, as is usual in Ponge, is that things should be allowed to speak for themselves, that the poet must take it upon himself to describe things from their own point of view.

We are caught once again in a vicious circle of aesthetics, the insoluble problem of anthropocentricity. If Ponge does not always confront this problem squarely, in this text at least he concedes that to be a human being capable of writing about the nonhuman in the latter's own terms is a form of perfection, and is impossible. If it were a realizable goal, then each poem would please each and everyone, indiscriminately, just as do "objects of sensations." But this cannot be: "Il y a toujours du rapport à l'homme. . . . Ce ne sont pas les choses qui parlent entre elles mais les hommes entre eux qui parlent des choses et l'on ne peut aucunement sortir de l'homme" ("There is always a relationship to man. . . . It is not things which speak among themselves but men who speak among themselves about things, and one cannot in any way get away from man," *T*, 189). This is an important statement; it is Ponge's admission, reiterated in many pages of his work, that all he can hope to do is to achieve some sort of relative success in his ambitions. The word "relative" in this respect crops up quite often in his writings.

The link between reason and resonance is established by the image of a vibrating chord, or just an abstract vibration, a link which Ponge puts epigrammatically in "Notes premières de l'"Homme"': "Une certaine vibration de la natures s'appelle l'homme" ("A certain vibration of nature is called man," *T*, 245). What he means, as he shows in *Pour un Malherbe* (143), is that a successful piece of writing produces the same "trembling of the taut string" as a correctly played lyre. Both resonate in an equally convincing way. Earlier in the same book, he gave a neat formulation of the "raison/réson" parallel: "Mais cette raison, qu'est-ce, sinon plus exactement la *réson*, le résonnement de la parole tendue, de la lyre tendue à l'extrême" ("But this reason, what is it if not more precisely the *réson*, the resonance of the taut word, of the lyre string stretched as tightly as possible" *P*, 97).

Predictably, the idea of harmony enters this discussion. Ponge suggests, some pages later, that "raison/réson" subsumes a perfect harmony of word and meaning: "Raisons, résons: un concert de vocables, de sons significatifs. . . . Jubilation de la note fondamentale dans la variété et l'audace de ses harmoniques (Pour cela, il faut qu'elle soit très tendue et vibre très fort)" ("Reasons, *résons*: a concert of words, of significant sounds. . . . Jubilation of the basic note in the variety and boldness of its harmonics [For that, it must be very taut and must vibrate strongly]," *P*, 133). Ponge is aiming, in his creative work, to achieve that harmony which would give it a necessity and validity. In many pages in his book on Malherbe, he expresses his great admiration for the classical poet, precisely because, traditionally considered uninspired, dry, and conventional, Malherbe has expressed a "raison française," by which Ponge means the most appropriate, the most necessary language (rhetoric, perhaps) for his times: "Henri IV et Richelieu firent venir Malherbe. Linguistiquement c'était justifié: une raison française, s'exprimant selon la langue française. Toute autre solution absurde" ("Henry IV and Richelieu paved the way for Malherbe. Linguistically it was justified: a French reason, expressing itself in accordance with the French language. All other solutions absurd," *P*, 141). There is a strong sense of history and continuity which often emerges in Ponge's writings, and it can be largely attributed to his belief in himself as the inheritor of Malherbe in this century. Certainly, he says quite clearly that he too is working towards "une raison française" (*P*, 106), which, says Sollers, is particularized by its binding relationship with the silent world of objects.[26]

E. *"Adéquation"*

As has been suggested, consideration of Ponge's aesthetics, in particular where they concern the object-status of language and the idea of a harmony between language and the world, inevitably leads to the concept of "adéquation," arguably the central point of Ponge's poetics, around which all other issues pivot. Because of this importance, a brief example of how "adéquation," or equivalence, works in a creative text was given in the introductory chapter; a fuller examination of it must now be undertaken. The first mention Ponge makes of "adéquation" comes early in *Méthodes*: "Genre choisi: définitions-descriptions esthétiquement et rhétoriquement adéquates" ("Chosen genre: definitions-descriptions which are aesthetically and rhetorically equivalent," *M*, 20). Here, Ponge is attempting some sort of working definition of the type of text he wants to write, which will not be just descriptive, or definitive, but which will surpass these functions of the dictionary by being set in the new rhetoric of equivalence. This rhetoric, as Higgins points out, will force the reader into a new awareness of the objects under scrutiny.[27]

From the first mention of equivalence in *Méthodes*, it is clear that the concept is going to run as a leitmotiv through both theoretical and creative texts. A few pages further on, Ponge, talking about that object of his attention in one of his longer and most successful pieces, "Le galet," in *Le Parti pris des choses*, offers "mon galet que je veux remplacer par une formule logique (verbale) adéquate" ("my pebble which I want to replace by an equivalent logical [verbal] formula," *M*, 26). It is interesting that Ponge brings together the idea of logic and language, reminding us of his occasional statements of faith in a scientific approach (see, for example, *Pour un Malherbe* [57]). Furthermore, the use of "formule" is reminiscent of the last sentence of "L'huître" in *Le Parti pris des choses*, where the use Ponge makes of the noun has implications about the "formula" available to the oyster, that is to say, a linguistic formulation in a poetic text. When Ponge says that he wants to "replace" the pebble by its equivalent formula, the choice of verb is significant, because he does not mean that his text will be a symbolic reference to the pebble, but rather that it will be the necessary correlate of it in language, a kind of nonidentical twin. If it were an identical twin, it would be indistinguishable from the object itself, and this is neither what is intended nor possible.

Ponge is ambivalent about the use of the calligram, one of the major endeavors to create this close resemblance, practiced in France in this century above all by Apollinaire. While he approves of it, hesitantly, he sees his own work as going beyond the restrictions of this particular form (see *Méthodes* [36, 216]). This ties in with Ponge's pronouncements about the inner logic and patterns of logic (the "fess-point"); language is not meant actually to reproduce the geometric shapes of objects, rather it must act in accordance with its own laws. This is the gist of a couple of important pages in the latter part of *Méthodes*: "Il faut que les compositions que vous ne pouvez faire qu'à l'aide de ces sons significatifs, de ces mots, de ces verbes, soient arrangées de telle façon qu'elles imitent la vie des objets du monde extérieur" ("It is necessary that the things which you can compose only with the help of these significant sounds, these words, these verbs, be arranged in such a way that they imitate the life of objects in the external world," *M*, 276). The crucial phrase is "imitate the life of objects." It is a question of rendering objects in an equivalent language, not, as the calligram seeks to achieve, the breaking of the inner laws of language, literally distorting it to make a picture with it.

In a somewhat imprecise way, Ponge goes on to speak of the "equivalent" text as one in which there is "un complexe de qualités aussi existant que celui que l'objet présente" ("a complex of qualities just as existent as the one which the object presents," *M*, 277). To make his point more fully, he goes on to talk about a hypothetical poem about an apple. It is not enough, indeed it is counter-productive, for the poet to exclaim that he loves the apple so much that he "wants to get inside it." Rather, "il est question d'en faire un texte, qui ressemble à une pomme, c'est-à-dire qui aura autant de réalité qu'une pomme. Mais dans son genre. C'est un texte fait avec des mots. Et ce n'est pas parce que je dirai 'j'aime la pomme,' que je rendrai compte de la pomme. J'en aurai beaucoup plus rendu compte, si j'ai fait un texte qui ait une réalité dans le monde des textes, un peu égale à celle de la pomme dans le monde des objets" ("it is a question of making a text out of it, which resembles an apple, that is to say which will have as much reality as an apple. But of its own kind. It is a text made with words. And it is not because I might say 'I love apples' that I will give an account of the apple. I will have given a more proper account of it if I write a text which has a reality in the world of texts, more or less the same as that of the apple in the world of objects," *M*, 277).

This is as good an explanation of "adéquation" as Ponge gives anywhere in his theoretical writings. The need for this equivalence is not a selfish promotion of the poet's new rhetoric, but rather, as Ponge claims early in *Méthodes*, a condition essential to the proper rendering of what he calls the "évidence" (the manifest presence) of things. It is as though to eschew "adéquation" necessarily leads the writer into the traps of the old, false languages, into the various kinds of poetic self-advertisement.

Apart from creative texts in which "adéquation" is shown at work, Ponge does discuss some precise, nonhypothetical cases. Those which he brings up in *Méthodes* are illuminating, both because they reveal how the process operates, and also because "adéquation" is shown to be very close indeed to the technique of the calligram, and even to be singularly "précieux." Talking of his poem on the apricot (in *Pièces*), he says that he intends to shape the letter *a* in such a way as to make it resemble the apricot as closely as possible. Similarly, of his piece on the goat, "LA CHÉVRE" (also in *Pièces*), Ponge says that the grave accent on the *è* is very important as it is the verbal equivalent of the goatee beard of that animal. If this is precious, it is pleasantly so, and inoffensive. However, the claims for equivalence made regarding the title of one of his long texts, "Le verre d'eau," are more grandiose and frankly ridiculous. For two pages, Ponge draws out every conceivable nuance from these words of the title; the opening v, the final u are held to be the only letters which resemble the shape of a glass. The *-er* and *-re* of "verre" have a perfect symmetry, and reflect each other as if they had been placed one on the inside, one on the outside of the glass; and if one were to shout out the r sound in "verre" in the presence of a glass, then it would splinter, demonstrating that essential characteristic of the object, its fragility.

Ponge continues in this way. It is excessive, the ingenuity displayed loses its value in this precious verbal game. What equivalence would Ponge be able to find in the g and the s of "glass of water"? Similarly preposterous seems the idea which he puts forward in *La Seine*, in which he proposes that the text proper should be set out in the restricted central portion of the page, leaving two large white spaces on either side of the print, which would thus be the river banks where the text is the Seine itself (*T*, 558-60). Just before this, Ponge had written: "Allons, pétrissons à nouveau ensemble ces notions de fleuve et de livre! Voyons comment les faire pénétrer l'une et l'autre!...Confondons, confondons sans vergogne la Seine et le livre qu'elle doit devenir!" ("Come on, let's mould together again these notions of river and book!...Let's merge together, merge together without shame the Seine and the book which it must become!" *T*, 557). Ponge seems to have forgotten his own principle concerning the inner and separate laws of language; he is favoring much more a calligrammatic game. The same may be said of his notion, put forward in his essay on the sculptor Giacometti, "Joca Seria," that a life-size statue should not weigh more than the real-life model (*N*, 67).

So, Ponge's practical examples of equivalence given in his theoretical texts do have the virtue of showing what the concept means, but the disadvantage too of being over-elaborate and precious. Fortunately, in the purely creative texts there are many fine examples of convincingly integrated equivalence. Some of these will be examined later. To return for a moment to the matter of theory, Ponge has a few pages in *La Seine* on the analogy between poems and liquids. He says (*T*, 533) that he will realize the equivalence of his texts in terms of liquids rather than solids, an idea suggested by his contemplation of the river, because they, his texts, like liquids, are half-way between the formless and the rigid (539). His text, like the Seine, will be "discours," a word which obviously affords a play on the "course" of the river (541-2). More interestingly, perhaps, Ponge says that the written text offers letters, shapes which make it come close to the thing signified, that is, to objects in the external world, just as liquids are very close to solids (538). The idea seems to be that texts are moving, changing things whose trajectory is constantly towards the solid fixity of the things to which they are bound by meaning.

A number of critics have made comments on "adéquation" in Ponge's work. Georges-Emmanuel Clancier, in his chapter on Ponge in *La Poésie et ses environs*,[28] speaks of Ponge's poetry as "necessity," because "en elle nom et chose ne feraient plus qu'un" ("in it, name and thing are meant to be one and the same"). Both Sollers and Higgins draw attention to a feature of equivalence often encountered in Ponge, namely that "sometimes the structure of an entire text is equivalent to the object,"[29] while an example of this total "adéquation" might be seen in "L'ARAIGNÉE" (in *Pièces*), a text typographically arranged to suggest the spider, a technique reminiscent of Mallarmé.[30] Sollers also has a good sentence on the overall effect of equivalence: "Ces phrases polies, solides, qui tendent à reproduire la forme et la constitution de ce qu'elles expriment, qui cernent l'objet et souvent le déséquilibrent pour marquer son entrée dans l'équivalence verbale; ces phrases mnémotechniques..." ("These polished, solid phrases, which tend to reproduce the form and the constitution of that which they express, which encircle the object and often throw it off balance to mark its entry into verbal equivalence; these mnemotechnic phrases...")[31] Sollers makes a telling point when he says that Ponge's language can throw the object under examination off balance.

A feature of Ponge at his best is precisely this ability not so much to capture the reader's imagination as to awaken in him new powers of observation by some startling insights. The final word on the practice of verbal equivalence should be left to Ponge himself, who, writing in "Texte sur l'Électricité" about those poets who put emphasis on it, says that he has always sought to join the ranks of those poets, and that he believes that he has succeeded in a small way, as he has the honor of generally being considered an exponent of the technique.[32]

In a comparatively early text, dating from 1929-1930, Ponge makes a statement about the necessity for the writer to "resist words," to say only what he wants to say, and this, an "act of public welfare," he calls a "rhetoric" (*T*, 177). The whole of his theoretical writings may be seen as having tended all along to a new rhetoric, this word being used fairly loosely by Ponge to mean a distinctive style, an authentic poetic voice. In view of what he consistently says, he cannot be using "rhetoric" to denote "eloquence," although its other meaning of "persuasion" might be more appropriate. In this text, he suggests that a new rhetoric should be founded, but he immediately qualifies this by adding that is a matter rather of teaching everybody the art of founding their own rhetoric. His emphasis seems squarely placed on the notion of an individual poet's voice, which may appear at odds with another important statement on the same matter, this one in *Méthodes*: "si j'envisage une rhétorique, c'est une rhétorique par objet, pas seulement une rhétorique par poète, mais une rhétorique par objet" ("if I envisage a rhetoric, it is a rhetoric per object, not only a rhetoric per poet, but a rhetoric per object" *M*, 260). This is a direct echo of a very similar statement made much earlier in *Méthodes*: "chaque objet doit imposer au poème une forme rhétorique particulière" ("each object must impose on the poem a particular rhetorical form" *M*, 36). It is apparent how dependent on the notion of equivalence Ponge's new rhetoric of objects is. What he means is that a poem's form must be determined by its subject (or object); the laws which govern the functioning of things must find their equivalent in a text similarly organized in accordance with laws of necessity: "Ce mécanisme d'horlogerie c'est la rhétorique de l'objet. La rhétorique, c'est comme cela que je la conçois" ("This clockwork mechanism is the rhetoric of the object. This is how I conceive of rhetoric" *M*, 260).

   A number of critics have evaluated the concept of rhetoric in Ponge's work. Léonard[33] sees it as a means adopted in order that Ponge may fulfill his wish to break away from the domination of ideas. This in turn is part of Ponge's aim to establish, through his descriptions and words, a relationship between man and the world, allowing him ultimately to pierce through to the essential. (Léonard cites Ponge's phrase about aesthetically and rhetorically equivalent definitions-descriptions.) Thibaudeau[34] considers Ponge's rhetoric to be very close to a classical rhetoric in letter and spirit. Clancier[35] takes rhetoric to be synonymous with an unpoetic language, and says that while Ponge does have a rhetorical slant, he is a genuine poet because he goes on beyond rhetoric, and enters the realm of emotion, love, fervor, all of which are drawn out of him by his involvement with the objects he is writing about. Finally, Sollers[36] writes of "un rhétorique pongienne, seul didactisme peut-être de notre littérature moderne; [d'] une enquête permanente sur les ressources et les possibilités de la langue...le langage devenat le tain réalité dès lors admise à nous exprimer" ("a Pongian rhetoric, perhaps the only didacticism of our modern literature; a permanent enquiry into the resources and the possibilities of language. . . language becoming the silvering of a reality henceforth allowed to express us"). This useful image of the silvering on a mirror—human beings looking at the outside world and being given back the image of themselves through language—may have been suggested to Sollers by Ponge's poem "Fable" (in *Proêmes*), a hermetic little piece whose meaning seems to have to do with the world/mirror analogy (*T*, 144).

III   *A Modern Classicism*

Ponge's large number of writings on poetics leads him away from false languages and voices, toward the necessary language which replaces them, and to his new rhetoric. The last section of this chapter must draw in all the strands and try to determine whether Ponge fits into any recognizable literary tradition.

Consideration of "adéquation" is important in this respect because, in that it concerns issues of content and substance as well as of language and style, it says a lot about what Ponge is saying, and not merely how he is saying it. This, of course, is scarcely surprising when one recalls that Ponge wishes language to be substance, to exist autonomously. In one of his earliest declarations of aesthetic belief made in *Méthodes*, Ponge declares that existence for him means the literary creation, or perhaps recreation, of the external world (14). He must mean by this that activity of allowing a correctly operating language to mirror the world of objects. His use of the verb "refaire" in *Proêmes* enhances this meaning. In the space of four pages, he brings in this verb three times, the last possibly being the most useful here: "A la vérité, expression est plus que connaissance; écrire est plus que connaître; au moins plus que connaître analytiquement: c'est *refaire*" ("Truly, expression is more than knowledge; writing is more than knowing; at the least it is more than knowing analytically: it is *remaking*," *T*, 228). This is reminiscent of the microcosm/macrocosm relationship of the text and the world.

In the same pages, Ponge supports his view by introducing the term "metalogic" and using it to designate a linguistic creation, by definition man-made, which parallels the "logic" of the object or thing described. "La poésie" is at one point quite simply seen as "*la création métalogique*" (*T*, 219); and a little later, he talks of his metalogical power to remake the world (*T*, 224). The function of this metalogic, according to Georges Garampon, is to facilitate a "résurrection dans le vocable de sa vertu objective" ("resurrection in the words of its [the object's] objective quality").[37]

Ponge has created a phrase, already mentioned, to contain the notions of metalogic, of re-creation, and of equivalence, indeed the broad sweep of his poetics. The formula "définition-description-oeuvre d'art littéraire" establishes the tripartite basis of an aesthetic seeking to blend the functions of the dictionary and the encyclopaedia with the creative process. Ponge does have a considerable preoccupation with the place of dictionaries in a literary aesthetic. His references to the Littré are numerous; he even maintains that this dictionary should be the poet's principal source book. His aim, nevertheless, is to go beyond the dictionary and similar books: "Il faut que mon livre remplace: 1° le dictionnaire encyclopédique, 2° le dictionnaire étymologique, 3° le dictionnaire analogique (il n'existe pas), 4° le dictionnaire de rimes (de rimes intérieures, aussi bien), 5° le dictionnaire des synonymes etc., 6° toute poésie lyrique à partir de la Nature, des objets etc." ("My book must replace (1) the encyclopaedias, (2) the etymological dictionary, (3) the analogical dictionary [it does not exist], (4) the dictionary of rhymes [of internal rhymes as well], (5) the dictionary of synonyms etc., (6) all lyric poetry, from Nature, objects etc. onward," *M*, 41).

If this seems a dry and austere program, one must recall Ponge's hostility to the sentimental and self-centered excesses of lyrical and analogical modes, and to all outworn poetic languages. Instead, his aesthetic strongly posits a poetic writing which will lie midway between definition and description. Clancier[38] sees this slightly differently; for him, Ponge's writing is situated somewhere between the dictionary and alchemy. Presumably, he is reaffirming the traditional belief in poetry as in part magical and indefinable, a belief which Ponge himself wants to reject. Again, Ponge's unsentimental emphasis on a factual basis for poetry brings to mind his somewhat hesitant theory that poetry is a science: "La Poésie est alors la *science* la plus parfaite, non la Mathématique, ni la Musique. Tout ceci, senti intuitivement par moi, est encore trop confus, il me faudra y revenir et essayer de préciser" ("So Poetry is the most perfect of *sciences*, and not Mathematics nor Music. All this, intuitively felt by myself, is still too muddled, I shall have to come back on it, and try to be more exact," *P*, 137).

No really clear exposition of this idea does occur; but the implicit notion of perfection, of laws, and of objectivity are taken up more fully in the several mentions Ponge makes of classicism. Not surprisingly, it is in his book on the great classical poet Malherbe that Ponge makes his clearest statements about it. In an important paragraph, he says that he has always considered that classical texts—those which by definition have proved that they maintain their significance and their interest—would be his only models. He has always thought that these texts had at least as much passion, sensitivity, and nuance as romantic or impressionist ones, but had also, thanks to a taming of these elements as well as to a particular arrangement of them, the supreme quality of indestructibility and impassive indifference to the vicissitudes of the four elements, qualities which characterize inscriptions, those permanent testimonies in stone (*P*, 188). Of the mutations of the classical idea, the one Ponge prefers is the baroque, so long as it remains properly ingrained in stone.

By the end of the seventh section of *Pour un Malherbe*, Ponge has moved to a partial definition of classicism: "Ce qui rend classique, ce n'est nullement la modestie, c'est le désir de convaincre et l'expérience du ridicule et de l'inefficacité du déchaînement, c'est le sentiment de la force de persuasion de l'*unique*, du *simple*, du *rigoureux* (voire du gracieux). C'est un *surcroît* d'orgueil qui rend simple, et un redoublement de ténacité ET DE RESSOURCES qui permet de faire d'obscurité, clarté" ("What makes for the classical is not at all modesty, but the desire to convince and the experiencing of the ridiculous and of the uselessness of the overflow of feeling, it is the feeling of the strength of persuasion in the *unique*, the *simple*, the *rigorous* [even the gracious]. It is an *increase* of pride which produces the simple, and a redoubling of tenacity AND OF RE-SOURCES which allows darkness to be turned into light," *P*, 285).

When, later, he says that he likes the rule which corrects emotion (310), the picture is completed of a personal classicism which conforms to the general dictates of classicism in that its imperative is to be sober, measured, and constantly objective, in Ponge's special sense, which is to say in the service of the object and not of the poet. What this classicism means in practice is a precise, sometimes laborious, picking of and picking at words. It is a process which aims at accuracy and a high charge of significance, but which, when it fails in this endeavor, can result in pedantry. Examples will be given later; it is enough to point out here that Ponge's almost obsessive concern with etymologies, the roots which he mentions when dealing with the "objeu," is both his strength and his weakness. A strength when he forces the reader to look anew at a word, in all its rich history, and at the object it denotes; a weakness when he contrives the most precious conceits around a particular etymology. For one critic at least, Ponge is a modern, and unexpected, classic for having undertaken a successful "défense et illustration de la langue française," to borrow the title of the celebrated call by Du Bellay in 1549 for a new sort of poetics.[39] Any novelty which may exist in Ponge's own poetics nevertheless rests solidly on the substructure of Latin word derivations. He has had a debt of gratitude to the Latin language ever since his childhood, because it is what has given the feeling of "depth" to French.

A. *Malherbe*

Ponge's classicism leads inevitably to a consideration of the reasons for which he admires Malherbe, whose standing as a poet may not be as considerable as his historical role in the evolution of French prosody. *Pour un Malherbe* may be considered both as a study of the poet and as an apologia for Ponge himself; if anything, the case for the latter looks stronger. Nevertheless, there does emerge from the book, if not a scholarly critique of Malherbe, at least an overall picture of Ponge's reasons for admiring him.

One of the clearest of these reasons comes early in the book, and is neatly aphoristic: "C'est le dictionnaire en ordre de fonctionnement" ("He is the dictionary in working order," *P*, 26). This is reminiscent of Ponge's declared aim to write a kind of literature which will both embrace and replace the dictionary; a literature whose usage of words will always work on the basis of their definitive solidity in the dictionary. So Ponge continues: "C'est le langage absolu. . . . C'est la beauté mathématique *plus* la matière des choses, éprouvée par la sensibilité et amenée à raison. C'est l'ordre mis dans les pierres. C'est la justification des mots et de la parole, sans coefficient d'esprit fin, spirituel, gracieux, joli, gai ou triste" ("His is the absolute language. . . . Mathematical beauty *plus* the substance of things, experienced by sensibility and brought to reason. He is order put into stones. He is the justification of words and the word, without any coefficient of delicate, clever, graceful, pretty, gay or sad wit"). Some of the main features of Ponge's poetics are recognizable here. The beauty of mathematical order (what Ponge later calls his "musique pythagoricienne" [*P*, 137]), the solidity both of objects and of language (Malherbe is the "dungeon" of French literature, Ponge writes [*P*, 241]), the contempt for trivial and gratuitous displays of brilliance. Ponge esteems Malherbe really for the very reasons that many others find him dull and pedestrian. Where they might look for expansive and lyrical effusion, Ponge finds "des monuments utilitaires" (*P*, 138). Ponge does not hesitate to place Malherbe alongside Cervantes, Góngora, Shakespeare, and Francis Bacon. The comparisons may seem a little unusual, but Ponge considers Malherbe an immortal, not just a great classical or preclassical figure. He is someone who transcends historical frontiers (*P*, 145).

Another epigrammatic statement about Malherbe comes a little later in the book, and uses a verb which Ponge repeats in similar contexts: "Il désaffuble la poésie" ("He strips poetry of its disguises," *P*, 58). This laying bare goes hand in hand with what Ponge sees as Malherbe's scorn for "Literature" with a capital *L*, and with the respect for strict rules of prosody which he shares with Ponge: "Dans la mesure où Malherbe dédaignait la Littérature, tout en lui assignant des règles on ne peut plus strictes, il est très proche de nous" ("Inasmuch as Malherbe was scornful of Literature, while assigning to it the very strictest rules, he is very close to us [Ponge]," *P*, 80). Malherbe's prosodic lawmaking involved the alternation of masculine and feminine rhymes, of which Ponge approves, although he himself, as a writer predominantly of prose poems, does not observe this rule. He approves of it partly because, as he says, the importance of the mute *e* in French accords perfectly with the importance of the feminine element *always* found in France (*P*, 227).

In short, Ponge has the highest regard for Malherbe because of the latter's sense of proportion ("chaque parole y a sa dimension juste"; "each word has its exact dimension," *P*, 13, 96) and because of the "absolute" quality of language which Ponge detects. Language is seen as stone, carved into solid and durable shapes which end up as utilitarian monuments to themselves: "Quelle vénération ne lui devons-nous pas d'avoir consacré son existence entière à travailler cette langue, à en ordonner les termes et à l'installer, pour ainsi dire, en une série de chefs-d'oeuvre qui ne concernent rigoureusement qu'elle!" ("What veneration do we not owe him [Malherbe] for

having devoted his whole life to working this landscape, to ordering
its elements and to installing it, so to speak, in a series of
masterpieces which strictly concern only that language!" *P*, 167).

A comment each by two critics about the relevance of Malherbe
to Ponge are worth mentioning here. Wider[40] assesses the meaning of
the "dictionary" idea, and concludes that Ponge has such an
unbridled admiration for Malherbe because Malherbe was able to
make poetry identical with the word itself, he was able to bring out
nature hidden in the dictionaries. Thibaudeau[41] sees a correspondence
between Ponge's rules about the "parti pris" and Malherbe's technical
imperatives—rare and sterile rhymes, cesuras, no hiatus, sense-units
in single stanzas, regular sonnets etc.—both writers thus joined
across three centuries by a common bond of classicism.

B. *"Relative Success"*

Ponge's concern to achieve a new classicism based on the rhetoric
of equivalence and on the primacy of the object might lead one to
the understandable conclusion that he is a dispassionate writer,
coldly antihuman, exercised only by questions about absolutes in a
nonhuman world. This is not so; a counterbalancing strain of
modesty bred of an acceptance of limitations, as well as an affirmation of a real interest in man, runs through Ponge's theoretical
works as it does through his creative texts.

He has made two major and apparently contradictory statements
about what he calls "relative success" in literature. The first, in
Proêmes (*T*, 205-10), dates from 1941-1943, the second, in *Méthodes*,
from 1952. In the first, prompted by his reading in 1941 of Camus's
Le Mythe de Sisyphe in manuscript, he considers the particular
conception of the absurd proposed by Camus, and concludes that the
lesson of strength and hope (which Camus does not quite draw,
according to Ponge) is that a *relative* success can be achieved by
human beings in the face of their absurd condition. A key word is
"measure." Ponge thinks it is crucial in this context, although
he does not really explain it. However, the word appears to be
about the harmony man can achieve with the world if and when he
uses language properly. In so doing, Ponge implies, he scores a
"relative success," which, like that of Sisyphus, gives him dignity
through an unflinching acceptance of what it is to be human. Wisdom,
continues Ponge, lies in being content with this, and in not becoming
ill with "nostalgia" (Camus's idea of a nostalgia for the absolute).

He then proceeds to a statement which combines this wisdom about the relative and the impulse towards the absolute: "Il faut concevoir son oeuvre comme si l'on était capable d'expression, de communion, etc., c'est-à-dire comme si l'on était Dieu, et y travailler ou plutôt l'*achever*, la limiter, la circonscrire, la détacher de soi comme si l'on se moquait ensuite de sa nostalgie d'absolu: voilà comment être véritablement un homme" ("One must conceive of one's work as if one were capable of expression, of communion etc., that is to say, as if one were God, and work at it, or rather *complete* it, limit it, circumscribe it, detach it from oneself as if one could not care less about one's nostalgia for the absolute: that is how to be truly a man," *T*, 207). Some paragraphs later, he applies this judgment to Sisyphus: "Sisyphe heureux, oui, non seulement parce qu'il dévisage sa destinée, mais parce que ses efforts aboutissent à des résultats relatifs très importants" ("Sisyphus happy, yes, not only because he can look his destiny in the face, but because his efforts end up by giving very important relative results," *T*, 209).

Ponge is a writer in the absurdist tradition insofar as his quest for harmony subsumes a constant desire to express himself and the world, and a constant falling short in this endeavor. He in fact equates the absurd with his position in the relative. Solace is to be derived from the heroism of making the attempt to achieve harmony, and, like Sisyphus, of doing so again and again. Language has a utilitarian function; the poet's Sisyphus-like dignity may lie in merely restoring this to language—Ponge offers as an example of this function the most utilitarian of phrases, "pass the salt"— thereby making a move toward establishing a harmony between man and the world (*T*, 209). Elsewhere in *Proêmes*, Ponge reaffirms his belief in the relative, inasmuch as a preoccupation with questions of the absolute, questions which remain insoluble, are a total waste of time. Much earlier in the same volume, Ponge had written: "Divine nécessité de l'imperfection, divine présence de l'imparfait, du vice et de la mort dans les écrits, apportez-moi aussi votre secours" ("Divine necessity for imperfection, divine presence of the imperfect, of vice and of death in writings, bring me also your help," *T*, 146).

However, there are at least two occasions, both in *Méthodes*, on which Ponge apparently contradicts this ready acceptance of limitations and qualified success. Firstly, he writes: "Tout simplement nous n'acceptons pas d'être DÉFAIT par: 1° La beauté ou l'intérêt de la Nature ou, à vrai dire, du moindre objet. Nous n'avons

par ailleurs aucun sentiment d'une hiérarchie des choses à dire; 2°
Nous n'acceptons pas d'être défait par le langage. Nous continuons
à essayer; 3° Nous avons perdu tout sentiment de la réussite
relative, et tout goût de l'admettre. Nous nous moquons des critères
habituels." ("Quite simply, we do not admit to being DEFEATED by
(1) the beauty or the interest of Nature, or, to be honest, of any object
at all. We do not have moreover any feeling about a hierarchy of
things to say; (2) We do not accept defeat at the hands of language.
We continue to try; (3) We have lost all sense of relative success, and
any wish to accede to it. We are scornful of the habitual criteria," *M*,
199).

Perhaps this reads not so much as a contradiction of the position
developed in *Proêmes*, rather as a development from it, colored by a
certain impatience and a growing sense of poetic ambition and
strength. Certainly, this quotation from *Méthodes* shows Ponge
hostile to too easy concepts of beauty, and facile linguistic solutions
which a "relativist" might accept. Later in *Méthodes*, in a section in
which he is dealing with the question "Why write?", Ponge answers:
Pour faire quelque chose qui puisse être lu, relu, aussi bien par soi-
même, et qui ne participe pas de ce hasard de la parole" ("To create
something which can be read, reread, by oneself as well, and which
does not participate in the chance of words," *M*, 266). Ponge seems
to have made a commitment in favor of a quest for a poetic
absolute, reminiscent of Mallarmé's, at the expense of his earlier
relativist position.

C. *Old and New Humanisms*

Ponge's position about mankind is as ambivalent as that about
the relative; he adheres to a two-way division between what he calls
the "old humanism" and a new form of it; obviously, he favors the
latter. He wishes to leave behind the old, and the way to do this is to
be pulled away by objects: "je me fais tirer, *par les objets*, hors du
vieil humanisme, hors de l'homme actuel et en avant de lui" ("I am
being pulled, *by objects*, away from the old humanism, away from
contemporary man and ahead of him," *M*, 41). The rather
portentious and biblical tone of this extract is reinforced by a
quotation on the same matter taken from *Le Peintre à l'étude*:
"Voilà des objets à qui nous demandons, car d'eux *nous savons
l'obtenir*, qu'ils nous tirent hors de notre nuit, hors du vieil homme
(et d'un soi-disant humanisme), pour nous révéler l'Homme, l'Ordre

à venir" ("Here are objects of which we ask, because from them *we know we will obtain it*, that they should take us out of our darkness, out of the old man [and of a so-called humanism], in order to reveal to us Man, the order to come," *T*, 517-18). This is an imprecise, apocalyptic vision which Ponge never quite really brings to earth with practical details, apart from the clue that his new rhetoric of objects is what will lead away from the myopic self-centeredness of the old humanism, about which he talks acidly in the "Entretien avec Breton et Reverdy" (*M*, 292-93). Jerusalem, Athens, Rome have all handed on a belligerent and complacent pseudocivilization calling itself humanist.

The unsentimentality of Ponge's position should not mask the deep emotional involvement which he says he has with man: "Non que je quitte...l'homme....Mais sans doute m'émeut-il trop, à la différence de ces auteurs qui en font le sujet de leurs livres, pour que j'ose en parler directement" ("Not that I am abandoning...man ....Without a doubt he moves me too much, unlike those authors who make of him the subject of their books, for me to dare to speak of him directly," *T*, 530). There is an echo of this unease in *Proêmes*, in which Ponge shows that his coyness is due, in part at least, to the difficulty he finds in making man a subject for his writing; he is not easy to place in the domain of the objective (*T*, 243). Ponge's apparent ambivalence about man stems from the fact that while he, Ponge, is proposing the seeming eclipse of man, he also wants at the same time to reconcile man and the world (*M*, 192, 195). But more than this, he is asking that man withdraw from the center of the stage in order that the material world may literally cool down again, and its mechanistic system function properly once more. Only when man recognizes that he has no greater significance on this planet than do all its other constituents will he be able to move freely toward Ponge's new humanism. Recognition of his rightful role will involve man's characteristic as a maker and user of tools, as the species which can harness certain natural forces, making of him, for example, a modern Ariel able to turn the power of electricity to his advantage ("Texte sur l'électricité," *L*, 177, 181).

More than this, however, the new humanism by definition means the achievement of self-coincidence, which is at the root of Ponge's thinking about man, and which he affirms at the end of his text on the snail. Just as the snail secretes slime and its own shell, so man, to obtain the same "measure," must learn the lesson taught him by the snail, and secrete "language and morality"; this is "humanism" (*T*,

61). The harmony within the new man living in full self-coincidence, and which Ponge likens to the smooth-running ("le régime") of a motor (*T*, 210), will make him "pure and simple," the herald of the new classicism: "C'est à un homme simple que nous tendrons. Blanc et simple. Nouveau classicisme" ("It is to a simple man that we will lead. Clean and simple. New classicism," *T*, 246).

CHAPTER 3

Poetic Practice

THE intention of the last chapter has been to sift through Ponge's abundant pronouncements on poetic theory, scattered throughout his work, and to separate them, as far as it is legitimate to do so, from what might be termed his poetic practice ("poetic method" would be misleading, given the title of one essay, "My creative method," and of the book *Méthodes*, both of which deal with more than just the practical questions of technique). What Ponge has said about the practice of poetry is less substantial than his discussions of theory, possibly because often he starts with the former but moves quickly into the latter. This chapter will look at Ponge's poetic practice as revealed by his comparatively few statements about it, and by his finished poems.

I *"Etymological conceit"*

The notion of equivalence, central in Ponge's poetics, depends so much on a nonutilitarian view of language—despite his concept of the poet's Sisyphus-like role of restoring a utilitarian function to language, discussed above—that it should come as no surprise that one of his most distinctive stylistic features should be the conceit. This word implies ingenuity and wit in the formulation of an idea or an expression, qualities undeniably present in a lot of what Ponge has written. But it also connotes the strained, the far-fetched, the cleverly hollow, "gongorisms" which are equally hard to ignore in Ponge. He has a predilection for forms of paranomasia, in particular what might be called the "etymological conceit,"[1] one that is fashioned out of the etymons of the given words, a process often involving puns, and which is adduced by Ponge as an instance of equivalence in action. The importance he attaches to etymologies calls to mind Heidegger's "word-mysticism" (Wortmystik").

On a number of occasions, Ponge spins a long phrase, a sentence, or even a paragraph, composed of an analogy, or simile, so tightly woven that the whole thing seems to be an extended pun. The opening of "Les mûres" (in *Le Parti pris des choses*) is one such; another is the first paragraph of the long "Texte sur l'électricité" in *Lyres,* a work commissioned by the Compagnie d'Électricité to accompany a technical brochure aimed at persuading architects to incorporate electricity into their building plans: "Pour nous conformer au style de vie qui est le nôtre depuis que le courant électrique est à notre disposition, nous établirons le contact sans plus attendre et jetterons brusquement la lumière sur nos intentions" ("In order to conform to the style of life which is ours since the electric current has been at our disposal, we will establish contact without further ado and throw some light on our intentions," *L,* 145). This is rudimentary; the ambitions of the wordplay are not great or serious. All depends on the possibilities of the phrases "établir le contact" ("to switch on the current," and, in its general application, "to make contact," here, with the reader); and of "jeter la lumière," which has exactly the same literal and metaphorical meanings ("to cast light upon") in English as in French.

Ponge becomes more subtle in the following paragraphs. Having set the tone in the first, he can then slip in, almost unperceived, words which suggest electricity while having a more normal nonspecialized meaning. Thus, in the second paragraph, he writes of "la vie courante," "ordinary life," where the adjective "courante" suggests the word for electric current. In the third paragraph, Ponge writes of men's habits which "shock." At the same time as slipping in these devices, Ponge is elaborating an argument, a form of intellectual, global "adéquation," in which he contends that the substance of his text on electricity will be intellectual (illuminating, he might have said), because, just as one seeks to turn on a light when one enters a darkened room, so an intellectual enlightenment is desirable at the outset in a book whose subject is so intimately connected with light.

Ponge's abiding concern with the etymologies of words—constantly he is demonstrating that the importance and the strength of words lie in their roots—is well exemplified ten pages further on in the "Texte sur l'électricité." Musing on the word "électricité," he first accepts that it derives from "Electron," because yellow amber was so named in Greek. But, more than this, Ponge wants to know *why* yellow amber was *justly* (*justement*) called Electron. To explain this curiosity, he adds "tout le passé de la sensibilité et de la connaissance m'y semble inclus" ("all the past in the matter of sensibility and of knowledge seems to me to contained in them [the words]," *L*, 155). There then follows the invocation of Electra, Prometheus, Thales, the Danaides, Lynceus, and others, all mythological figures loosely brought together by their various suggestions of fire, light, lightning, and water. All, in short, embodiments of the attributes of electricity.

An insight both into the obsessive concern Ponge has for the history of words and into the near-mystical way in which they thrust themselves into his consciousness is provided in an examination of the word "sacripant" in *Méthodes*:

> Prenons-nous en flagrant délit de création.
> Nous voici en Algérie, tâchant de rendre compte des couleurs du Sahel (vues à travers la Mitidja, du pied des monts Atlas). Il s'agit donc là, dans une certaine mesure, d'une besogne d'expression.
> Après beaucoup de tâtonnements, il nous arrive de parler d'un rose un peu *sacripant*. Le mot nous satisfait *à priori*. Nous allons cependant au dictionnaire. Il nous renvoie presque aussitôt de Sacripant à Rodomont (ce sont deux personnages de l'Arioste): or Rodomont veut dire Rouge-Montagne et il était roi d'Algérie. C.Q.F.D. *Rien de plus juste.* (*M*, 23-24)

> Let's be caught red-handed in the act of creation.
> Here we are in Algeria, trying to give an account of the colors of the Western Sahara (seen across the Mitidja, from the foot of the Atlas mountains). It is therefore a question, to a certain extent, of a task of expression.
> After several fumblings, we happen to speak of a somewhat *swaggering* pink. The word has an *a priori* satisfaction for us. Still, we look it up in the dictionary. Almost straightaway, it refers us from "Sacripant" to "Rodomont" (they are two characters in Ariosto): now Rodomont means Red-Mountain, and he was king of Algeria. Q.E.D. *Nothing more just.*

When Ponge deals again with this incident (*M*, 282), he adds that he felt vindicated in refusing the other words which were crowding his mind until the luminous arrival of this one which meant "red mountain of Algeria." Whatever Ponge may say against inspiration in a writer, this incident, and the way it is recounted, come very near to betraying a belief in it—unless the felicitous "docking" of idea with word discloses some would-be scientific law of correspondences which a logically-minded poet has worked hard to master.

The types of conceit exemplified so far in this chapter depend on the association of ideas, and on puns, even extended ones. More frequently, one encounters in Ponge conceits which are whimsically built on a free association whose impetus is either etymologies or

even the pictorial (calligrammatic, almost) possibilities of individual
words. The result can be clever, but unconvincing, because Ponge
tries to persuade us that what are random examples of wordplay are
really epistemological truths. Thus, in "Prose à l'éloge d'Aix,"
Ponge makes an astonishing assertion about the name of this old
town in Provence: "L'A y représente la montagne Sainte-Victoire.
L'I, des eaux éternellement jaillissantes. L'X enfin, un séculaire
croissement de routes, comme aussi la croix mise en ce lieu sur
certaine entreprise barbare" ("The *A* represents the Sainte-Victoire
mountain. The *I*, the eternally springing waters. The *X*, finally, an
age-old intersection of routes, as well as the cross put in that place
during a certain barbaric enterprise, *L*, 126). This near-calligram is
markedly precious, and has the characteristics of a *post hoc propter
hoc* reasoning. The letters of "Aix" have the good fortune to be
sufficiently pliable for Ponge to impose on them certain qualities
which he claims are essential, when surely they are entirely
accidental. There seem to be two major points here: one, that the
system of pictorial identities implicit in this example would have to
be universally applicable to be serious, and two, what Ponge sees in
the word's letters is distinctly subjective. While the letter *X* may
easily suggest a cross, it is much more arbitrary to assert that an *I*
corresponds to flowing water. If there is a strength in this type of
conceit, it is that it can force the reader, through its surprising and
oblique approach to things, to look afresh, to clear away the clutter
of habitual responses to a word. Occasionally, this is effected with
economy, as when Ponge says that the word "cageot" (packing-
crate") is halfway between "cachot" ("dungeon") and "cage."
Happily, this correspondence between a scale of objects and a scale
of sounds works on this occasion.

Ponge can be long-winded when a similar enterprise turns out to
be more awkward. He confesses that he finds the task of defining the
mimosa (definition meaning the establishing of convincing links
between sound and sense) anything but easy, and he devotes
eighteen pages to the problem. The text of "Le mimosa" (*T*, 305-24)
is a major example in Ponge's work of the process of definition at
work; he incorporates the notes toward the definition, the various
stages and attempts, the several assaults on the plant, made from
different approaches. So, the final text contains, among other
exercises and essays, a short but elaborate double acrostic of two
tercets; the association of "mimosa" with "mima"; an association of
the mimosa with a lady's petticoat, and with Italian comedy, and
thereby a linking of mimosa with pantomime; and a quantity of

definitions taken straight from the Littré dictionary, of which the most significant are "mimosa" itself, "mimeux" (of sensitive plants which contract when touched), "eumimosa" (apparently another shrub). All are etymologically tied together through Latin "mimus," because the plants concerned seem to grimace like a mime when they contract. Ponge builds up a cumulative definition of the mimosa, going over the same ground several times, but slightly changing the perspective on each occasion, all the while focusing an intense light on the word itself, as much as on the botanical object it represents (and, incidentally, showing how the concept of the "en abîme," the "fess-point," works), until the "dictionary in working order" is felt to be as complete as it can be.

Although "Le mimosa" has its tedious and pedantic sides, it does have the virtue of convincingly placing the mimosa, as a plant and as a linguistic object, firmly in the center of the reader's consciousness. The seriousness of the poetic task, its successful aspects, overcome the moments of pretentiousness. The risk of relying on conceits to support the whole weight of a text is that they will collapse because of their inherent weakness which is that generally they can only be ornaments on a structure whose solidity has been established by other means. This becomes apparent in one brief sentence from *Pour un Malherbe*, in which Ponge would have us believe that the name "Malherbe," through a false etymology, tells us real things about the bearer of that name: "Quelque chose de mâle (malherbe), de libre (mauvaise herbe)..." ("Something male [malherbe], something free [weeds]...." *P*, 12). This is merely a sleight of hand, with which Ponge wants to persuade us, as he does elsewhere in the book by more orthodox means, that Malherbe was both stongly masculine and temperamentally free, unconcerned with the niceties of gracious attitudes; "mauvaise herbe" means a "ne'er-do-well," an "outsider," as well as "weed."

Ponge's puns can become totally frivolous; Mozart is referred to as "l'amodoué Mozart" ("the alluring Mozart," *L*, 127), a play on one of this composer's forenames, Amadeus. Or they can lead, as has been shown in the previous chapter, to the coining of new words: "patheuse" (*T*, 211), which presumably is compounded of "pathos" ("bathos," "bombast") and "pâteux" ("clammy," "dull," "cloudy"). When Ponge deliberately gives individual words their full etymological significance, thereby enlarging the range and the force of these words, he is especially convincing. He fills out language with a richness and a density, which, after all, is a characteristic of any good poet. An unspectacular example is to be found in "Le gymnaste" (*Le Parti pris des choses*), whose final phrase runs: "et c'est alors le parangon adulé de la bêtise humaine qui vous salue" ("and then it is the adulated paragon of human *bêtise* which salutes you," *T*, 72). The whole of this poem will be considered in the next chapter; it is one of Ponge's most successful and typical. Here, the point of interest is the word "bêtise," impossible to translate in this context by one word alone. Normally, it would mean "stupidity"; but Ponge uses it to close a poem which has turned a human being, the gymnast, into a performing animal, a nonhuman circus act. And so we are compelled to register the etymology of "bêtise," that is, something which pertains to an animal ("bête").

Ponge can be more sophisticated than this. In the "Réflexions en lisant 'L'essai sur l'absurde'" (*T*, 210), he uses the noun "*cure*" (Ponge's italics) in, as he says, its Heideggerian sense of "souci" ("care," "worry"). This does not show any great concern with etymologies, just an awareness of a precise usage. What is interesting, however, is that he had used the adjective "curieux" in a poem from *Le Parti pris des choses*, "L'huître" (*T*, 48); with hindsight, we can reasonably assume that he intends it to mean more than the obvious "inquisitive." For, if we take it to include the meaning of "careful," with implications of "fastidious" and "cautious," then the phrase "Les doigts curieux s'y coupent," meaning that fingers which are both inquisitive and careful are cut when trying to open an oyster, takes on a pleasing dimension of humorous irony.

In his "Le verre d'eau" Ponge relies on a correct etymological meaning to further his definition of water. It hinges on the verb "désaltérer," "to quench thirst." Likening drinks to a beloved woman, he writes: "Il est des bien-aimées qui désaltèrent et altèrent à la fois: ainsi du vin. Mais l'eau ne fait que désaltérer. Si l'on est altéré, elle vous désaltère, c'est-à-dire vous restitue en votre identité, votre moi" (There are some beloved who quench thirst and alter [one] at the same time: so it is with wine. But water only quenches. If one is thirsty, it takes away one's thirst, that is to say it restores to one one's identity, one's self," *M*, 129). Ponge's point is that to get at the true meaning of the verbs "désaltérer" and "altérer," one must scrutinize their etymologies. Of course, the root word is Latin "alter," "other," and so the idea of thirst has its origin in one of the observable results of being thirsty, namely, that a person becomes changed, is temporarily "not his usual self," or can even become "beside himself," or can "take leave of himself." So, Ponge implies in his eulogistic pages about water, this life-bearing liquid not only is a pleasant refreshment, or something so common that it is given little attention, but in fact a vital agent of psychic integrity. This example demonstrates effectively a point constantly made by Ponge; that a proper respect for a word, a complete familiarity with that word, with all that has happened to it, and with all the layers of significance it has acquired, enable one then to approach the object, the quality, which the word denotes in the clear knowledge that one is thus going to reach the truth about it. It is in this respect that Ponge's contention that a word does not symbolize a thing, but is intimately part of that thing, makes sense. The more one knows the word, the more one knows the object.

The critic Jean-Luc Lemichez has drawn attention to at least two important and sustained examples of Ponge's use of the etymological conceit.[2] He takes the opening paragraphs of Ponge's "La crevette dans tous ses états" (*Pi*, 15-17) and brings to light just how frequently Ponge uses sounds and words which echo "capra," the Latin root of "crevette"—thus "capricieuse," "capricorne," "capon," etc. Then Lemichez turns his attention to "Le pré" (*N*, 201-9), in particular to a section which is constructed as a stanza on the homonyms of "pré":

> Crase de paratus, selon les étymologistes latins,
> Près de la roche et du ru,
> Prêt à faucher ou à paître,
> Préparé pour nous par la nature,
> Pré, paré, pré, près, prêt,
>
> Le pré gisant ici comme le participe passé par excellence
> S'y révère aussi bien comme notre préfixe des préfixes,
> Préfixe déjà dans préfixe, présent déjà dans présent.

> Crasis of paratus, according to the Latin etymologists,
> Close to rock and to water-course,
> Ready to be mown or grazed,
> Prepared for us by nature,
> Meadow, adorned, meadow, near, ready,
>
> The meadow lying here like the supreme past participle
> Is revered here just as is our prefix of prefixes,
> Prefix already in prefix, present already in present.

> (*N*, 205; Francis Ponge, *Nouveau Recueil*, Éditions Gallimard;
> translated by Martin Sorrell)

One of Ponge's most marked practices in his development of the etymological conceit is all too manifest in this extract. Not content to ring the changes on the obvious homonyms, he enlarges his scope to include words which contain the sound, with the result perhaps that many readers will feel a sense of annoyance at what quickly changes from a serious etymological assessment into a counting game which could go on *ad nauseam*, and which soon ceases to say anything of substance. In fairness, the extract quoted constitutes about one half of a verse piece in which Ponge seeks to make the point that this monotonous repetition of one syllable correctly echoes the monotony but at the same time the variety of the real world. Nevertheless, the whole venture seems to illustrate the risks of preciosity. However, Ponge's readiness to play verbal games at the slightest prompting can have embarrassingly gauche results— see, for example, the play on "Lancashire" and "encachées *here*" in "L'anthracite" (*Pi*, 71).

Thibaudeau[3] also has a page on Ponge's conceits. His general point is that Ponge's texts are simultaneous accounts of the origins both of words and of things. He illustrates this with a reference to "L'huître" (already mentioned in this chapter for its use of "curieux"). This very title, says Thibaudeau, permeates the whole of the poem by virtue of its circumflex accent, which Ponge has maintained in the "-âtre" suffix of certain words—"blanchâtre," "opiniâtrement," "verdâtre," "noirâtre."[4] This technique is a more delicate version of what was found in "Le pré": it takes the art of juggling with homonyms and puns into the domain of accent marks.

Certainly, there are far too many examples in Ponge's work of puns and plays on sounds and words to be listed here. It will be sufficient to mention just one or two. The title of one poem in *Le Parti pris des choses*, "La desserte du sang bleu," probably involves a pun on "desserte," which can mean both "broken meat" and "the duties of an officiating clergyman," and in the context of a rather difficult poem, both seem relevant. Then, in *Proêmes*, Ponge gives the title "Pelagos" to one of his short poems, and this is probably a play on "Pelasges," the French for the prehistoric Pelasgian people of the Eastern Mediterranean, who are thought to have occupied Greece before the Hellenes, while etymologically the title relates to "deep," "abyss," "gulf," and "pool" (compare "Archipelago"). Finally, the noun "expression" and the verb "exprimer" take on a richer than normal significance in Ponge; in "L'orange" (*T*, 46), "expression" is used in the first sentence deliberately with its quite rare meaning of "squeezing." as well as that of "verbal expression," which is Ponge's aim in the poem. Similarly, "exprimer" is used in a double sense in a discussion of how a forest manifests and communicates its existence: "Chacun de ses efforts pour s'exprimer a abouti à une feuille..." ("Each of its efforts to express itself has resulted in a leaf...," *M*, 250). The tree in the forest conveys information about itself by means of a leaf; it also squeezes, or projects out of itself, by forming a leaf, which is the end product of the sap's movement to the extremities of the tree, as the "expression" of the orange is the juice's bursting of that fruit's limits.

Whatever the reader may feel about the value in poetry of an unrelenting quest for etymologies, Ponge has made it a cornerstone of his orthodoxy, every bit as binding as his love of the natural world: "Comme j'aime à dire que ce qui me plaît dans la nature, c'est son imagination (devant tel paysage, telles lumières, devant tel produit naturel, tel organisme, telle pierre, si je m'écrie: 'C'est beau!' C'est comme je dirais: 'Ah! par exemple, je ne l'aurais pas trouvé tout seul! Je n'aurais pas inventé cela')—ainsi de la nature enfouie dans les dictionaries: des mots, ces pierres précieuses, ces merveilleux sédiments" ("Just as I like to say that what pleases me in nature is its imagination [before such and such a landscape, effects of light, before such and such a natural product, an organism, a stone, if I cry out: 'It's beautiful!' It is as if I said: 'Ah! now I wouldn't have been able to find that on my own! I couldn't have invented that']—so with nature hidden inside dictionaries: so with words, these precious stones, these marvellous sediments," *M*, 120).

II "*Description through Negation*"

Turning now from etymological approaches to particular words, to methods used in organizing complete texts, a distinctive aspect of Ponge's technique is what Higgins calls "description through negation,"[5] and which might be expanded to include "description in terms of differences." That is to say that a certain number of Ponge's texts which seek to be a "definition-description" (most typically in *Le Parti pris des choses* and *Pièces*) follow a pattern of negative comparisons—what the object under consideration is *not*, or does *not* resemble—comparisons which are rejected until, it is hoped, at the end of this paring away, the object itself finally emerges and stands on the page, unique and unencumbered. This technique may be considered a function of the process of eidetic reduction. It is interesting to note that Ponge considers that to write about the differences between things is to advance beyond the restrictions of the analogical mode in poetry. He deals specifically with this matter in a page of "My creative method," in which he consigns analogy to the poetic "magma," the amorphous and viscous residue, which, although he uses it, he also discards. Ponge continues: "Les analogies, c'est intéressant, mais moins que les différences. Il faut, à travers les analogies, saisir la qualité différentielle. Quand je dis que l'intérieur d'une noix ressemble à une praline, c'est intéressant. Mais ce qui est plus intéressant encore, c'est leur différence. Faire éprouver les analogies, c'est quelque chose. Nommer la qualité différentielle de la noix, voilà le but, le progrès" ("Analogies are interesting, but less so than differences. It is necessary, through analogies, to capture differential quality. When I say that the inside of a walnut is like a burned almond, this is interesting. But what is still more interesting is their difference. To be able to make people feel analogies, that is something. But to name the differential quality of the walnut, that is the goal, that is progress," *M*, 41-42).

Ponge's creative writings contain examples, perhaps not in all a very great number, which bear this out. In *Le Parti pris des choses*, the short "Rhum des fougères" contains this paragraph: "Ni bois pour construction, ni stères d'allumettes: des espèces de feuilles entassées par terre qu'un vieux rhum mouille" ("Neither wood for building with, nor cord wood for matches: kinds of leaves heaped on the ground and moistened by old rum," *T*, 40). The initial description through negation gives way to an affirmation, and this movement in the pattern of description is quite typical of Ponge. Thus, in "Escargots," he says that the snail does not resemble the swine (having established in the previous paragraph that the snail is "the friend of the ground," to which it adheres with all its body); nor does it have the swine's mean little trotters, its worried fashion of trotting along. However, in the next paragraph, Ponge moves to the affirmative by means of a straightforward and vivid analogy, a mode which he in no way eschews, despite some claims to the contrary. The snail is said to glide slowly forward "tout comme un long navire, au sillage argenté" ("just like a long ship, with a silvery wake," *T*, 60).

It does seem from the negative comparisons that what Ponge is in fact achieving is a positive statement. He suggests that a comparison between an object and something else is not valid, and yet the terms of that comparison generally are close enough to charge the original object with a greater degree of life and clarity. This, of course, is the force of a well-wrought analogy, and it may be considered that Ponge is effectively a traditional maker of analogies, only thinly disguised. To take one sentence from "La grenouille": "A peine viande ses muscles longs sont d'une élégance ni chair ni poisson" ("Scarcely meat its long muscles are of an elegance neither flesh nor fish," *Pi*, 60). Ponge lists three things which the frog is not, and yet it is close to all of them, so that when the frog's long and elegant muscles (the affirmative part of the sentence) are juxtaposed with the idea of meat, of flesh and of fish, we get the impression of having come as close as is possible to the essence, the definitive truth of the frog, even though it may ultimately remain elusive. In fact, this fine little poem finishes on an uncomplicatedly affirmative note.

"Les poêles," however, (a few pages on in *Pièces*) ends with a sentence, standing as a separate paragraph, which closes the poem apparently on a negative tone, yet again it contrives to say something constructive about the subject: "Les rapports de l'homme à son poêle sont bien loin d'être ceux de seigneur à valet" ("The relationship between man and his stove are very far from being those of master to servant," *Pi*, 65). The introduction of the master and servant figures is surprising; Ponge tells us in effect that the comparison is not appropriate, yet the final outcome is that a new dimension, fresh and gently witty, is revealed, one which does add some definition to what a stove is.

It might be possible to argue that the more indistinct or amorphous the object, the more recourse the writer will be obliged to have to analogical modes. Ponge has not shied away from problems of this sort; he has written in various texts about water, while one piece, concerned with the viscous rather than the liquid, bears the unlikely title of "Ode inachevée à la boue". It is a fairly long text, and investigates a variety of aspects and effects of mud in an attempt to reach a definition of it. Incidentally, Ponge makes his ode "equivalent" to mud by transposing its formlessness into the "muddy," incomplete trailing off of the concluding lines; the ode is unfinished precisely because mud, by its very nature, has no clear contours, no beginnings and endings. As far as an analogical method is concerned, there is one interesting passage in the middle of the ode: "Quand nous parlerons de l'homme, nous parlerons de l'homme. Et quand de la boue, de la boue. Ils n'ont, bien sûr, pas grand-chose de commun. Pas de filiation, en tout cas. L'homme est bien trop parfait, et sa chair bien trop rose, pour avoir été faits de la

boue. Quant à la boue, sa principale prétention, la plus évidente, est
qu'on ne puisse...aucunement l'informer" ("When we will speak of
man, we will speak of man. And when of mud, of mud. They obviously have very little in common. No affiliation at any rate. Man is much
too perfect, and his flesh much too pink, to have been made out of
mud. As for mud, its principal, its most manifest claim is that one can
do nothing with it, that one can...in no way inform it," *Pi*, 70).

Ponge's thoughts, focusing first on mud, are led to the elemental,
to the earth and dust which compose human bodies; but this
comparison between mud and man is rejected. However, by this
point, the analogy has taken root in the reader's mind, and he is able
to throw each of the terms into sharper relief as a result. Man is not
mud, and vice versa. The comparison is invited and tested; it is
found to be wanting, but it has yielded just a little more knowledge,
not only about mud, but possibly about man as well. The passage
concludes with a typical wordplay on "informer," which skillfully
links man and mud. For mud will not, unlike man, receive
information, as obviously it is not intelligent. At the same time, also
unlike man, mud cannot have form. Part of its essence is that it is
viscous, and can only take on the shape (the "solidity") of an object
which contains it, or on which it is spread. Man's difference in this
respect is conveyed by the word "parfait," which Ponge is using
etymologically to convey not moral worth in man but the fact that
he is completely "made" or "finished." Richard[6] devotes some
attention to this ode, and also makes the valuable point that when
Ponge is scrutinizing things with a view to defining them, he picks
out as their "critical zones" their frontiers, their limits and fringes. It
is contours which define. Ponge focuses his attention in the "Ode
inachevée à la boue" on archetypes of the definite (bodies) and of the
indefinite (mud).

III   *Poem Endings*

Allied to the issue of how to define things, how to give them
verbal form by exploring all their possibilities until a more-or-less
complete picture has been built up, is the role of the poem ending, to
which Ponge attaches considerable importance. Analysis of his
creative texts will reveal that very often the last line or paragraph is
not just a tidy conclusion but the moment of release at which the
object finally surrenders to the poet and reveals itself. Quite literally,
the end of a poetic text is the moment when the object is named, is

captured in language, and when therefore the act of writing becomes complete, and need not proceed. The idea of "writing against language" has some relevance in this matter; the poet must write in order to overcome the resistance, the secrecy of language, and the moment of his victory is marked by the appearance of the definitive word.

In one of his theoretical texts, Ponge considers the place of the poem ending: "Et voilà une autre façon de tenter la chose: la considérer comme non nommée, non nommable, et la décrire *ex nihilo* si bien qu'on la reconnaisse. Mais qu'on la reconnaisse seulement à la fin: que son nom soit un peu comme le dernier mot du texte et n'apparaisse qu'alors. . . . Ou n'apparaisse que dans le titre (donné après coup)" ("And here is another way of tempting the thing: consider it as unnamed, unnamable, and describe it *ex nihilo* so that it becomes recognized. But recognized only at the end: so that its name should be somewhat like the last word of the text and should appear ony then. . . . Or should appear only in the title [given afterwards]," *M*, 35).

In his article on Ponge, Sartre sees the typical structure of Ponge's poems as rapid, mobile, liquid at the outset, then coming to a conclusion with the major, condensed, climactic part which contains the "nomination" of the thing. This "nomination" does not necessarily mean the actual use of the appropriate noun itself— although this does occur at least once, with great effect, in "La gare," with its final line cutting short a piece of sustained and very colorful evocation: "C'est LA GARE, avec ses moustaches de chat" ("It's THE STATION, with its cat's whiskers," *Pi*, 79). Here, the definitive statement involves an enigmatic "poetic" image; elsewhere, Ponge makes more naked and unsupported statements, such as that in the phrase with which he ends "Pluie": "Il a plu" ("It has rained," *T*, 36). By using the perfect tense of the verb, Ponge situates the rain in the immediate past, completing, "perfecting" its description.

Perhaps the most common type of ending, however, is the one in which bald statement is replaced by a controlled, rich sentence, or sentences, whose function is to bring out the definitive aspects of the object. Thus, in one of Ponge's most engaging little poems, "Le papillon," a series of four paragraphs, all concentrating on particular features, behavior or stages of development of the insect, leads to the final paragraph which allows us to stand back from the minute examination, and to observe, with the help of an analogical phrase, the butterfly simply being a butterfly: "Minuscule voilier des airs maltraité par le vent en pétale superfétatoire, il vagabonde au jardin" ("Tiny sail-boat of the air, a superfluous petal battered by the wind, it roves around the garden," *T*, 62).

Very much the same technique is used in another poem about the animal world. The pigeon, which Ponge tries to capture in three stanzas, is finally "released" in a last sentence of sharp definition: "Puis envole-toi obliquement, parmi un grand éclat d'ailes, qui tirent, plissent ou déchirent la couverture de soie des nues" ("Then fly away obliquely, amid a great burst of wings, which pull, crease or tear the silk cover of the skies," *Pi*, 9). One is reminded of the suggestion, encountered earlier, that Ponge's objects are defined in terms of their contours, of the limits which separate them from other things. By juxtaposing discrete entities, showing what each object is *not*, Ponge makes us acutely aware of the uniqueness of an object. Here, the pigeon stands out against a sky into which it does not blend, but rather which it spoils by tearing it.

The ending of "La radio" gives a definition of a radio receiver, but does so by a conjunctive rather than the disjunctive technique found in "Le pigeon": "Fort en honneur dans chaque maison depuis quelque années—au beau milieu du salon, toutes fenêtres ouvertes— la bourdonnante, la radieuse seconde petite boîte à ordures!" ("Greatly honored in every house for the last few years— right in the middle of the lounge, all the windows open—the humming, the radiant second little refuse bin!" *Pi*, 100-101). The sheer presence of the radio is suggested by the lack of any active verb; then, it is defined with humor, pun, and association of ideas. The adjective "radieuse" obviously is a play on "radio," while "bourdonnante" conveys both the hum of sound and of electricity, and the buzz of flies scavenging in a wastebasket. The radio, like the basket, teems with the evidence of a life which, however, may be unwelcome, even unhealthy, in a person's living quarters.

As was the case with the "Ode inachevée à la boue," Ponge sometimes reflects in the endings of his texts either the amorphous- ness of an object or its average status, even its mediocrity. The whole of "Les olives" betrays Ponge's view (not an "objective" view, clearly) that the olive is moderately satisfying, but awkward (its size when being eaten, its stone) and a little bitter. After inviting us to put an olive in our mouth, Ponge concludes: "Voilà qui est tout simple. Ni de trop bon ni de trop mauvais goût. . . . Qui n'exige pas plus de perfection que je ne viens d'y mettre. . . et peut plaire pourtant, plaît d'habitude à tout le monde, comme hors-d'oeuvre"

("A very simple thing to do. A taste which is neither too nice nor too bad.... Which does not demand any more perfection than I have just given it... and can give pleasure, does normally please everyone as an hors-d'oeuvre," *Pi*, 111).

As a general rule, it might be said that the poem endings, insofar as they are of the sort which define the object, tend more in *Le Parti pris des choses* to the conceit than do those in other collections. Three examples will demonstrate this (the ending of "Le pain," a poem considered in the introductory chapter, would be a good further example). In "La fin de l'automne," the two terms of the title, end and autumn, are equally under discussion. Ponge evokes the deadness of nature, the shedding of all aspects of life, and by the penultimate paragraph, moving ahead of the cycle of seasons, he anticipates spring. So, in order to bring his poem to an end, to recall the finality in the title, and perhaps to keep in the foreground the autumn vegetation, especially wood, which has been the substance of the poem, his concluding paragraph turns away from thoughts of spring: "Mais là commence une autre histoire, qui dépend peut-être mais n'a pas l'odeur de la règle noire qui va me servir à tirer mon trait sous celle-ci" ("But here another story begins, which perhaps depends on but does not have the smell of the black ruler which I am going to use to draw my line under this one," *T*, 38). The elements of conceit center on "dépend" and on "règle noire"; "dépend" conveys both emotional, personal dependence, but also etymologically it means "to hang from," so that any further story about spring would come below the ruler which is drawing the finishing line of the present poem, while it would also be concerned with the rebirth of fresh-smelling vegetation, including the wood, at present still dead ("noire"), of which the ruler is made. The finality of autumn, the cycle of seasons, and the completion of a piece of writing are all moulded together in one terse sentence.

A conceit, precious and humorous, rounds off the poem "Le cageot." It is a comparatively short piece, neatly composed of three paragraphs all conveying the fragility of the materials and construction of a packing-crate used for fruit, etc. And so, precisely because the crate is fragile, destined for quick disposal, Ponge makes his poem light, rapid, and transitory, and ends it thus: "cet objet est en somme des plus sympathiques,—sur le sort duquel il convient toutefois de ne s'appesantir longuement" ("this object is in short one of the most agreeable—on whose fate it is right that one should not place too much stress," *T*, 43). The conceit lies in "s'appesantir," meaning "to insist," "to dwell on a subject," and "to become, to weigh heavy." Ponge will go gently with the crate; he will neither crush it physically nor wreck his verbal equivalent of it by being long-winded.

The final example from *Le Parti pris des choses* has the distinction of being doubly conclusive. The very last word of "Le galet" contains the full force of a conceit with which to complete the meaning of the poem; and the poem happens to be the last one in the collection. It is a long piece (twelve pages) in which Ponge obviously explores a vast area of approaches and permutations in a laborious attempt to fix, as usual, the essence of the particular object. It is a serious endeavor, undertaken with no apparent humor until the last paragraph. Here, Ponge, striking the moral note appropriate to a fable, turns away from the pebble to consider what he himself has been doing. He decides that his style has been too dependent on words, by which he must mean that he is getting in the way of the desired "self-expression" of the object. He is relatively pleased with what he has done in the poem, which he finishes: "Trop heureux seulement d'avoir pour ces débuts su choisir *le galet*: car un homme d'esprit ne pourra que sourire, mais sans doute il sera touché, quand mes critiques diront: 'Ayant entrepris d'écrire une description de la pierre, il s'empêtra," ("Only too happy to have thought to choose, for those beginnings, *the pebble*: for a man of wit will only be able to smile, but doubtless he will be touched, when my critics say: 'Having undertaken to write a description of stone, he got into a tangle,'" *T*, 115). The verb "s'empêtrer," taken in its first sense, would suggest that Ponge means that he found it impossible to accomplish the task of description which he had set himself. This meaning is strengthened when one recalls that one common usage of the verb denotes the process of becoming entangled in seaweed, thus providing an immediate association with pebbles on a beach. More than that, however, one would surely be justified in suspecting that Ponge has at the back of his mind Latin "petra" ("stone"), which, while not etymologically linked with "empêtrer," has clear echoes of it. This kind of false relationship would be tempting to Ponge, and would give an appropriate meaning to the last line of the poem, and in fact to the whole poem. That is, the poet took on the quality of stone, became stone, in the act of describing it, or perhaps in order to describe it. Seen in this way, the final statement of the poem turns the whole piece into a successful experiment in "adéquation."

There remains at least one important example of a definitive poem ending to look at. The last lines of "Le pré" (*N*, 209) come close to a calligram. Ponge asks in them that the typesetters who deal with this text about the meadow should draw a line under the final phrase, and then print "Francis Ponge" immediately below that line. In making this request, of course Ponge actually complies with it, and the end of the text consists of a line drawn under the last verse, with Ponge's name below. This elaborate piece of preciosity is designed to convey the idea of the end of the poem, the conventional signature found at the end of a piece of writing, but also, because the poem has been about a meadow and about the flora which abound on its surface, Ponge is bringing himself to an end, his task completed, by asking to be buried immediately below the surface of the meadow. Literally, "Francis Ponge" lies below his meadow.

IV   *The Place of Things: Their Categories*

So far, we have looked at certain structural and stylistic features in Ponge's approach to the things and objects which he has chosen to be the subject of his writing; things which are what he calls "prétextes," or "excuses" at the same time as "pre-texts" (*M*, 12). It would be appropriate now to consider both what Ponge has said himself about the place of things in his work, and the categories of things which interest him. His starting point seems phenomenological: "Notre âme est transitive. Il lui faut un objet..." ("Our soul is transitive. It needs an object...," *N*, 145) Very early in his writings on theory and method, Ponge indicates that his disdain of ideas and of the old values of poetry have led him to a confrontation with the exterior world, and to make what he calls an "inventory" and a "definition" of its objects: "je me consacre au recensement et à la définition d'abord des objets du monde extérieur, et parmi eux de ceux qui constituent l'univers familier des hommes de notre société, à notre époque" ("I devote myself to making an inventory and definition in the first place of the objects in the exterior world, and among them those which constitute the familiar universe for people in our society, in our time," *M*, 11).

Ponge has brought forward a loosely political reason, on top of any purely aesthetic ones, for concentrating his attention on the commonplace things of a thoroughly recognizable world; this sort of object is intimately bound to the contemporary average man. This is one of the more subtle ways in which Ponge's often covert anthropocentricity, if not humanism, displays itself. A page later in *Méthodes*, he writes that "*la variété des choses est en réalité ce qui me construit"* (*"the variety of things is in reality what constructs me"*), which might be equally applicable to the average man who may be defined in terms of the objects with which he surrounds himself, and for which Ponge has found equivalents in language (cigarettes, matches, bread, pieces of meat, eiderdowns, potatoes, anthracite, suitcases, radios, dogs, etc., etc.).

We are again brought face to face with one of the most difficult problems of Ponge's aesthetics, namely, how to reconcile his under-lying human and therefore, in both senses, partial viewpoint with his repeated claim that things must be described from their own point of view. Ponge's predilection for things commits him to the latter posi-tion, which he cannot always defend convincingly: "J'ai dit que la seule façon de nous exprimer authentiquement était de nous enfoncer dans notre différence,—de l'exprimer, à travers une matière traitée sans vergogne, non à partir de nous-mêmes mais à partir du monde,—et donc des objets les plus familiers, dont nous sommes le plus sérieusement imprégnés,—rendus avec l'intensité et la modestie qui leur convient" ("I have said that the only way of expressing ourselves authentically was to lodge ourselves firmly in our differences [from objects]—to express it, via material handled without any shame, not using ourselves as the starting point but the world—and thus the most familiar objects with which we are the most heavily impregnated—rendered with the intensity and modesty which befits them," *T,* 503).

This is a bold attempt to come to grips with the problem of viewpoints, but it cannot really be dispelled by phrases about the world as the starting point. Nor can the vague, somewhat mystical recognition that objects are issuing a silent plea that men should give them a voice ("la muette supplication, les muettes instances qu'elles font qu'on les parle...," *T,* 137). More helpful perhaps are the pages in *Méthodes* (268-70) in which Ponge, in fairly impassioned style, pleads on behalf of objects which again he sees as locked in, condemned by their lack of communications systems (we have to accept without argument this interpretation of what it is to be, as it were, animatedly inanimate) to be frustrated until the right poet takes notice. Not only does Ponge ask us to show pity and sympathy for a world which is seen very much as a paralysed body, but his marked interest in the visual arts, displayed in his various texts on modern painters and sculptors, links up with his poetics, for the way in which he apprehends the world is shown here as a predominantly pictorial one. The key is that things, according to

Ponge, are in a way "damned," and the poet must direct his efforts to absolving them. Their damnation is made apparent by color; if a thing is green, it is damned by being doomed in what Ponge assumes to be its aspiration to whiteness. It is unable to let green rays through, unlike a white object, which is white because it allows through all color rays. This "defect" contributes to a thing's individuality, as well as to its "dramatic" and "tragic" sense.

Ponge sees an awareness of this tragic element of things in the paintings of Braque, while Picasso, by contrast, conceives of colors as positive qualities which assert an object's choice. If an object is red, it is red because it has decided to be just that and no other color. Both of these approaches (Ponge obviously identifies more closely with Braque's) give a preeminent place to Ponge's "silent world of things," and restore to things those rights, defined elsewhere as "indefeasible" (*T*, 257-58), which he believes French poetry to date has denied them. Richard[7] sums up Ponge's attitude to things in this respect by saying that the condition of things—by extension, all the nonhuman world—is that their silence masks their desire to be incorporated by man into his world, achieved by expression in language.

It is of some interest to note that in another of Ponge's texts about painting, this one on Chardin and entitled "De la nature morte et de Chardin," he has as a main theme his pleasure in making a minute and detailed observation of things (*N*, 165-75). Again, the implication is that Ponge's attitude to objects corresponds most closely with that of a painter.

The somewhat emotive and sentimental view of things discernible in Ponge's invocations of Braque, Picasso, and Chardin may be considered as part of the near-mysticism which was mentioned earlier. In fact, Ponge follows his remarks on the two cubists with a paragraph in which he denies the charge of mysticism which he predicts will be leveled against him. He denies it by countering that what he is doing, in opposition to any mysticism, is to talk about things with honesty and appropriateness (*M*, 271). Nevertheless, elsewhere Ponge shows a distinctly religious reverence for things: "Mais alors, quels sont les véritables oracles? Quels sont ces oracles...qui demeurent éternellement disponibles pour l'inter-prétation. Ne serait-il pas justement autre chose que les énigmes, si parfaites soient-elles? Ne serait-ce pas *les objets*" ("But then, what are the true oracles? What are those oracles...which remain eternally available for interpretation. Would it not be precisely something other than enigmas, however perfect they may be? Would it not be *objects*," *M*, 239).

Things are oracular, they speak with a colossal force, so much so that, further on in the same essay, Ponge likens them to a bomb. The emphasis shifts from the mystical to the loosely political in a grandiloquent phrase: "Allons! Cherchez-moi quelque chose de plus révolutionnaire qu'un objet, une meilleure bombe que ce mégot, que ce cendrier" ("Come on! Find me something more revolutionary than an object, a better bomb than this cigarette butt, than this ash tray" *M*, 260). The mixture of an anarchic spirit with a wondrous attitude to the ordinary elements of life recalls surrealism, and the fact that Ponge was briefly a member of that movement. The subsequent lines talk of the "bomb" in terms of a clockwork mechanism, and this reveals an important aspect of Ponge's conception of the world. He writes: "il s'agit...d'un mécanisme d'horlogerie...qui, au lieu de faire éclater, maintient, permet à chaque objet de poursuivre en dehors de nous son existence particulière, de résister à l'esprit." ("it is a question...of a clockwork mechanism...which, instead of causing an explosion, keeps things working, allows each object to follow its own particular existence outside us, and to resist the mind").

In "Le galet," Ponge also puts forward the mechanistic view: "la nature apparaîtra enfin...comme une montre dont le principe est fait de roues qui tournent à de très inégales vitesses, quoiqu'elles soient agies par un unique moteur" ("nature will appear at last...like a watch which works on the principle of wheels turning at very unequal speeds, although they are moved by a single motor" *T*, 109). In *Pour un Malherbe*, the same idea is made absolutely explicit: "c'est à partir des machines qu'on peut apprécier à sa valeur la Nature, elle aussi une machine, une horlogerie, mais si grandiose, si nuancée, compliquée, variée à tel point!" ("it is on the basis of machines that one can appreciate Nature at its full value, for it also is a machine, a piece of clockwork, but so grandiose, so full of nuances, complex, varied to such a degree!" *P*, 74). Man himself, in Ponge's conception, is part of this mechanistic scheme: "j'ai songé à un poème évoquant le Monde où nous sommes plongés, où nous baignons comme un petit rouage, minuscule mais indispensable, ridicule mais précieux et sacré..." ("I thought of a poem evoking the world in which we are plunged, in which we swim around like a little cog, minuscule but indispensable, ridiculous but precious and sacred..." *P*, 74).

Among the critics, Sartre has drawn attention to what he sees as Ponge's process of turning human beings, such as the gymnast and the mother, both subjects of poems by Ponge, into behaviorist things,[8] while Higgins sees Ponge's mechanistic objects and creatures as characterized by their "involuntary forms of behavior."[9] Richard writes that Ponge breaks up objects into their constituent parts, but then brings them together again in an order which is more often than not mechanical rather than living.[10]

Furthermore, Sartre and Richard, as well as José Carner, have interesting things to say about the physical categories into which Ponge's chosen objects fit. Sartre claims that "le solide prédomine. Le solide et la science, qui a le dernier mot" ("the solid predominates. The solid and science, which has the last word").[11] Carner, in an article entitled "Francis Ponge et les choses,"[12] also sees Ponge's objects as solid, defining a "thing" as an exclusive but repeated form, unable to be folded over on itself, with the result that the only possible expressions of it are "quelques signes paralysés" ("a few paralysed signs"). Richard[13] seeks to demonstrate that Ponge's objects are characterized by qualities of discontinuity, punctuality, and insularity. (There would have to be a category of exceptions, surely, to allow for such texts as the ode on mud, the very model of the viscous, amorphous, and continuous). Some critics hold that Ponge prefers to deal with the surface of things; the inside or underneath of these things being formless and monotonous, surfaces have the beginnings of shape and contour, something by which to grasp the thing, its reality. Richard includes in his list of Ponge's well-contoured things the drop of water, the crumb, the snail, the pebble, the shrimp. The moral as opposed to the purely physical dimension of Ponge's objects can be attributed to their open, flourishing, and active nature, "une qualité interne d'épanouissement et d'ouverture." On the other hand, Sartre reaches a provisional conclusion in which he taxes Ponge with not having come to things with an "étonnement naïf," Ponge's own definition of his attitude, but with a "parti pris matérialiste."[14] In not being faithful to his word, Ponge has lost objectivity, as it were, by overemphasizing objects.

V *Preciosity and Pedantry*

Enough has already been said in the foregoing chapters about a number of negative characteristics of Ponge's theory and practice; it is necessary now merely to recall that preciosity, pedantry, periphrasis, and self-satisfaction creep into his work regularly, almost systematically. In some respects, of course, there is a case to be made out for their inclusion, and it has been seen that preciosity, for example, is one penalty of Ponge's approach to language. A further aspect of his method may be mentioned here, for perhaps it is related to the questions of preciosity and pedantry; Ponge has said that for him the act of writing is to be slow, deliberate, and regular: "Il me faut surtout...ne pas trop en écrire, très peu chaque jour et plutôt comme ça me vient, sans fatigue, va-comme-je-te-pousse" ("Above all I must...not write too much, very little each day, and rather as it comes to me, without tiring me, in an easygoing way," *M*, 16). Ponge has made a virtue of necessity, for, as he discloses in *Proêmes*, his social condition which obliged him to take an exhausting job left him with a mere twenty minutes each evening, before he finally gave in to sleep, in which to do his writing (*T*, 126). He also writes that part of his poetic method is what he calls an active contemplation (*M*, 254). All these statements seem to add up to a laborious and ponderous method, although it must be said that in a substantial proportion of his work (especially in *Le Parti pris des choses* and *Pièces*), laboriousness has produced some very tightly controlled and impressive writing.

At other times, Ponge can be prolix and loose, as if he were unable to achieve correct measure. However, a point is made by Higgins in this respect.[15] He draws attention to the fact that Ponge often leaves in his finished poems words, phrases, etc. which appear to be clumsy and unpolished, and which normally one would expect to find eliminated from the final version of a text. Vocabulary of conjunction is especially prevalent, but it is included, according to Higgins, because Ponge wants to stress the "intentional relation between subject and object." Thus, the seemingly unfinished can be as much part of Ponge's aesthetic as the polished and the well-wrought.

VI   Humor

There are grounds for thinking that, despite this ponderousness, and the tone of lofty endeavor, Ponge is not without humor. Certainly, his writings are full of wit, and Higgins talks of his irony.[16] But a more obvious humor does perhaps emerge as well. Richard[17] considers that the concept of the "objeu" is founded in a certain humor; it could be that it acts to check the precious excesses of unmitigated seriousness. Sollers[18] sees Ponge's ability to anchor his reader in his physical representation of reality while maintaining contact with reality itself as a kind of smiling but serious game in which humor has a crucial role. Blossom Douthat[19] suggests that Ponge's humor takes away the layer of seriousness imposed by utilitarianism, and that he achieves this largely by the use (reminiscent, it might be said, of Jules Laforgue in the nineteenth century), of invented humorous-sounding words, such as "amphibi-guïté." Jean Onimus[20] concedes that Ponge's descriptions contain humor, but that in the end this humor has tragic resonances, because it is only a mask which cannot go on hiding the great gulf of despair which the descriptions in fact create.

Whether or not this rather imprecise claim is valid, there are poems of Ponge's which not only have moments of humor but whose whole conception and execution are humorous. An excellent example is "Le Ministre" (*L*, 18-19), one of Ponge's "définition-description" pieces where "adéquation" in the first paragraph and mocking analogies in the remainder are deployed without any apparently serious claims being made: "Qu'une M, majestueuse porte cochère assise sur deux piliers à même le sol de la rue, à l'entrée de la tortueuse venelle SINISTRE décapitée d'abord de l'enseigne au serpent qui s'y dresse, modifie (en mugissement) le sifflement des souffles venant de gauche qui s'y engouffrent: de cette opération naît le MINISTRE" ("Let an *M*, majestic main door resting on two pillars at the street level, at the entrance to the tortuous SINISTER alley, with its decapitated crest standing there, formed of snake motifs, modify [into a bellow] the whistling of the breaths of air coming from the left and which are funneled there: from this operation is born the MINISTER"). This admirably ironical opening paragraph, capitalizing on the equivalences of the letter *M*, playing on "sinister" and "minister," pokes fun at the manner and bearing of a self-important minister who is about to pass through the imposing doorway like a gush of wind, or perhaps hot air. The poem concludes with a short and equally derisive paragraph: "Et bientôt les signatures processionnent comme des cafards sur les feuillets qui jonchent en désordre une table du mobilier national" ("And soon signatures march in procession like cockroaches on the sheets of paper which are strewn in disorder over a table of the national furniture"). This almost political satire gains much of its effect from the strength of the word "cafard," which also suggests "cant" and "humbug," a "sneak" in school, a "sanctimonious air," and, in the expression "avoir le cafard," "to be fed up" or "to be bored stiff."

VII   *Versification*

Consideration of "Le Ministre" will serve as a useful lead into the matter of Ponge's versification, if it can be called that, and about which a little need be said. "Le Ministre" is typical of the shape, length, and pattern of prosody which Ponge favors for his shorter (and, generally speaking, best-known) texts. Clearly, apart from a few scattered, usually early, poems, Ponge has dispensed with traditional arrangements by stanzas, with strictly measured line length, and with rhyme.[21] Instead, he has placed himself among the group of French poets, from Baudelaire onward, who have evolved the so-called prose poem. This said, it is difficult to assert that Ponge has any marked affinity with any of these poets outside this purely formal consideration. Perhaps his concern with the world of objects calls to mind his contemporaries Guillevic and Follain, but formally Ponge is not much like them. Rather, he is reminiscent (as has been said in the introductory chapter) of the *Histoires naturelles* of Jules Renard, and these *Histoires* are normally considered to be not poetry, but rather prose fables. If Ponge's texts often seem to be examples of tightly constructed prose, one reason is that, as he himself said, he is governed by imperatives and considerations which are too serious to allow him to stop over simply technical matters surrounding the laws of prosody. He quotes a few lines from Baudelaire in support of his attitude: "Rythme, parfum, lueur, ô mon unique reine!" ("Rhythm, perfume, gleam of light, o my only queen!") is the line which Ponge finds particularly telling, although he does not explain exactly why.

The indications are that he may not in fact be too far removed from the idea of a "poetic" style such as it is practiced in, say, Rimbaud's prose poems. In these, considerations of rhythm, internal rhyme, assonance, etc. are not neglected even if stanzaic patterns are abandoned in favor of sense groups. The way in which Ponge often organizes a text around a forceful last line or paragraph, with the rest of the text building up cumulatively to that ending shows, of course, a concern for controlled structures. More than that, however, Ponge works around certain phonetic relationships in a given piece, hovering around rhyme, but not embracing it nor eschewing it. Higgins[22] has pointed to such a relationship, in "L'orange," between "éponge" and "orange," showing that the similarities and differences between these two words are a paradigm of the objects they designate. The ways in which Ponge reveals himself as a craftsman not unaware of the established devices of prosody will become apparent in the next chapter, where individual texts will be analyzed in their entirety.[23]

Before that, there must be some discussion of two problematical issues of aesthetics which have periodically arisen in the foregoing chapters. The first concerns the nature and the place of the human dimension in Ponge's work, the second, the role of analogy.

VIII   *Human Presence*

Despite the fact that so much of Ponge's writing is about objects, human beings are treated occasionally, not only in those pieces which apparently have a dehumanizing effect, such as "Le gymnaste" and "La jeune mère," but also in the lengthy and ambitious "Notes premières de l'"Homme'," in *Proêmes*, whose loosely coordinated sections present man both in terms of behaviorism and as a species composed of varying individuals to whom Ponge can respond with a degree of warmth. His approach to man has some resemblance to that of Camus, to whom Ponge makes reference in the "Notes." A humanism of sorts is implicit at least in the task of writing about man. Furthermore, in the "Réflexions en lisant 'L'essai sur l'absurde,'" he seems to reveal himself as something of a humanist by showing that his concern is to find the way for man to realize himself, as a human being, a way which centers considerably on abandoning any quest for the absolute, and on settling instead for a situation in the relative. However, this Camusian warmth is by no means universal in Ponge's work. We have already seen that he reproaches the humanist tradition for its self-centeredness, to which could be added the comment made by Wider[24] that Ponge considers that humanism has not gone far enough in its exploration of the world, and is not motivated by the desire to be complete.

Ponge often opposes man and the nonhuman world, giving his sympathy to the latter. The possible danger of this division is that, on the one hand, Ponge will have nothing of value to say about man, and on the other, that he will overreach himself in trying to forget his humanity as he writes about the world of objects. It is a danger, which, as has been seen, he largely avoids by maintaining that the proper use of language can allow objects to emerge from the prison of their muteness, while at the same time the practice of language is what defines man, and makes him heroic, as Ponge writes in the last lines of section 4 of "Pages Bis" (*T*, 217). Oxenhandler[25] feels that Ponge is opposed to humanism, to "any position that gives man a privileged status in the universe," while Sartre[26] disagrees, saying that simply by speaking, Ponge is serving mankind.

However, the aesthetic problem remains. Whether or not Ponge reveals himself to be a humanist, he has to reconcile his "parti pris" for things with his human perspective. Phenomenology, a method first suggested by Sartre as applicable to Ponge, is most useful in effecting a reconciliation. The world is as it appears in the observer's consciousness, but it is susceptible of eidetic reduction. The intuition of an observer such as Ponge, while not eliminating human consciousness, will permit the essence of things to be disclosed. So, as Sartre says, Ponge's world is one in which man is present through his enterprises (and, of course, through its "presenter," Ponge), but from which he is absent as mind ("esprit") or as "projet."[27] This is the gist of Elaine Marks's helpful and less high-sounding comments in the introduction to her anthology of modern French poetry:[28] "man is defined in relation to the object. . . . The poet seeks to humanize the material world without attempting to assimulate it by means of analogy to his own private world." If this is so, Ponge has been able, while not negating his humanity, to avoid the trap of solipsism.

Gerda Zeltner-Neukomm[29] does not agree, however. Her claim is that, despite appearances, man is the real center of what Ponge is describing. When he allows things to reveal themselves, he does so solipsistically, and these things become toys for men to use, toys made of words. Zeltner-Neukomm concludes from this that Ponge is anthropocentric (revealed in his type of imagery), which is evidence that his real concern is to reestablish a binding and harmonious liaison between man and the exterior world. Ponge is thus finally seen as a poetic counterpart of the humanists Malraux and Camus, as well as of the existentialists.

Besides the moments of declared humanist feelings, besides the anthropocentric perspectives, Ponge gives evidence that man is his real concern even when the nonhuman appears to have most effectively eclipsed the human. His anthropocentric tendency is at its most pronounced in many pages of *Le Savon*, where soap is turned into a sentient being, intelligent of man's needs and playfully responsive to them (see especially *S*, 25-27, 87-89). In an article by Jean Grenier,[30] the contention is made that Ponge chooses to describe objects which are of the sort to interest human beings, and to be cataloged in man's inventory of such objects. Things are seen as adding to man; they are his dependents. In a way, this opinion tallies with a phenomenological reading of Ponge, for his objects are seen as the recipients of a kind of emotive intentionality.

The question of humanism, and of human perspectives in Ponge obviously exercises many critics; there appears to be no agreement among them on the issues. It would seem safe to say, however, that, apart from the matter of which subjects a given writer has chosen, and what his sympathies for them may be, the emphasis placed on certain stylistic devices—particularly the analogical modes of metaphor and simile—will reflect the extent of the subjective component of the writing. This is what Zeltner-Neukomm is saying, and it would be fruitful therefore to determine what place metaphor and simile have in Ponge's work.

IX   *The Place of Analogy*

In view of Ponge's wish to allow objects to speak for themselves, to have them reveal their essences, their naked truth uncontaminated by human intervention, it might be expected that he would avoid analogical writing. Elaine Marks[31] believes that Ponge does in fact steer clear of it, for its danger is that it would tend to negate the "en-soi" of objects, and render the exterior world too solipsistically. The point seems fair, although Marks's conclusion is questionable. In the first place, Ponge is not afraid of using the most direct type of analogy, namely, simile. Examples of straightforward comparisons are quite plentiful; the opening of "Le magnolia" serves as an illustration: "La fleur du magnolia éclate au ralenti comme une bulle formée lentement dans un sirop à la paroi épaisse qui tourne au caramel" ("The magnolia flower bursts in slow motion like a bubble slowly formed in a thick-sided syrup which is turning into caramel," *Pi*, 55).

The comparison is striking and successful; but it might be thought that it tells us more about the writer's imagination than about the magnolia. In terms of Ponge's aesthetics, would this not be inferior writing? If an object is meant to speak for itself, the conjuring trick which Ponge must perform surely should be to turn language back on to the object, in its own terms. Simile reveals all too frankly the intercession of a biased party, and would appear to work against the idea of equivalence. In fact, when Ponge does use simile to striking effect, as in the example from "Le magnolia," he seems to be an entirely orthodox writer, not afraid of trying to dazzle the reader with what is a conventionally contrived image. This leads one to conjecture that traditional poets, unashamedly using simile and other stocks-in-trade, may be just as well equipped as Ponge to render the reality of the phenomenal world. Good imagery will always provide sharper focus and a brighter light to bring out truth in whatever context. However, simile may have a particular place in Ponge's aesthetic in this respect: if his intention is to reach a single, definitive truth about a thing, the simile, by bringing together yet keeping apart that object and other things to which it is compared, will be wholly appropriate, because simile suggests that one thing is like another, of course, but at the same time it is not that other thing. Thus the first object remains fixed, solid; simile acts like a series of assaults from various sides, with the aim of penetrating through to the essence of the object.

Metaphor, examples of which very much outnumber simile in Ponge's work, acts quite differently. Critics, particularly Sartre, Higgins, Oxenhandler, and Wider, agree that metaphor is a cornerstone of Ponge's poetic method.[32] His metaphors, it might be argued, range from short, single examples, then to extended ones which run as a thread through sections of a text, even a whole text, and finally embrace the entirety of Ponge's work, in the sense that equivalence could be interpreted as the metaphorical relationship of world to language. Some of Ponge's metaphors serve the often moral aim of his texts. For example, on the two occasions when man is seen in terms of a mollusc, in "Notes pour un coquillage" (*T*, 86) and "Des raisons d'écrire" (*T*, 185), it is to establish that man's condition is to secrete language as a snail or a shellfish secretes its shell. In "Un rocher" (*T*, 167-68), the whole text is constructed around the metaphorical assimilation of rock and poem, concluding with an acknowledgment of the enormity of the task facing the poet who has to remove the (metaphorical) rock blocking his doorway. Sartre[33] holds that the description of purification in "La lessiveuse" (*Pi*, 80-85) is a metaphor of a deep-seated schema of purification which is embedded in human consciousness.

The two classic views of metaphor, Aristotelian and Platonic, are at the basis of Ponge's own. For Aristotle, the premises were that language and reality are separate entities, and that the manner of saying something does not materially affect or alter what is said. Therefore, metaphor was a technique of language which could be brought into play in order to clarify, or to add to our understanding of, reality. The Platonic view, however (and from which romantic formulations derive), holding that there was an "organic" relationship between metaphor and language as a whole, stood in opposition to Aristotle's notion that it could simply be applied and withdrawn from language proper as an extrinsic property. For the Platonic romantics, metaphor, as part of our process of imaginative thinking, was a crucial means of discovering the unity of all things, and their essences.[34]

Ponge seems to belong to both schools. In his desire to get away from the old rhetoric, from the "artistry" of writing, he shows perhaps a hostility to the Aristotelian position and its adherence to the idea that metaphor is something imposed by a clever writer, while his concern with the essences of things suggests a Platonic approach. In practice, however, Ponge's often very self-conscious writing, the abundance of conceits and preciosity, both of which are considerably bolstered by metaphor, would indicate an Aristotelian view that reality remains apart from the various ways a writer attempts to render it. In a sense, it could be said that if one believes that Ponge has succeeded in wedding exterior reality to linguistic expression, if, that is, "adéquation" works, he is a Platonist; but if, on the other hand, one finds that, despite his attempts to bridge the gap between objects in the world and objects in language by analogical, particularly metaphorical modes, Ponge has not made the two identical, then these objects remain apart in the way suggested by Aristotle.

On the question of how simile and metaphor operate in Ponge, one reason why he should favor metaphor so much is that it gives the feeling, or illusion, of getting close to an object rather more strongly than does simile. Simile respects the autonomy of the things being compared; metaphor moves further toward blurring the distinctions between them. Because Ponge is so involved, often emotionally, with his chosen objects, metaphor suits his approach more than does simile, the latter perhaps better fitted to a more dispassionate attitude. But a more fundamental reason for this predilection, one that has its roots in the full depth of Ponge's aesthetic, concerns the matter of relative as opposed to absolute success in his work. Oxenhandler has written that "by its very nature the metaphor implies the transparency and interchangeability of the names which we give to things."[35] The use of metaphor presupposes that its user believes that the truth about a thing is shifting, unfixed. A writer such as Ponge who heaps up a large number of metaphors is presumably conceding that he cannot hold the object still, and capture its essence; he is bound to settle for repeated assaults on the object, and for relative successes. Metaphor says that things *are* other things, evanescent, ungraspable.

Ponge's texts are so often a compilation of several approaches, each slightly different from the previous, to the essence of a thing; each time the "name" changes, if only a little. Despite some fine poems which seem to say more about an object than one might have thought possible, part of the reason why there is often a provisional feeling about Ponge's work may be that his predominantly analogical mode indicates that it is impossible to achieve an absolute in language, and that metaphor, far from taking us fully to the noumena of an object, puts us back instead on to the tentative paths taken in the approach to it. As Higgins points out, metaphor operates on the basis that all language is comparative, contrastive, and negatory.[36] In Ponge, metaphor as much as simile concedes that the nonhuman world remains irreducible. This, after all, is an old problem for any poet, and Ponge's rather rhetorical talk about allowing objects to speak for themselves in their own language cannot really seduce us into thinking that he has unearthed fundamentally new issues of aesthetics, nor that he has come up with radically new methods of confronting these issues. In trying to achieve identity of language and exterior world, Ponge has had to settle instead for analogy. While this has resulted in some fine texts full of acute observations, literally insights, it is safe to say that he has not broken truly new ground, struggling as he is in the trap of a language which he is attempting to make suit an object better than it suits himself.

However, Ponge's attempts to get the measure of things through metaphor can on occasions be stunning, and in a long poem such as "Le lézard" (*Pi*, 94-99) he has created and sustained a metaphorical interdependence of lizard and poem; the lizard emerging from the wall is a metaphor of the poetic act. This, incidentally, shows Ponge's tendency to write fables with an allegorical content. Ponge shows himself to be as forceful a maker of images as any poet. Nowhere is this more happily shown than in the ten pages of "L'asparagus," in which, typically, he has taken an unpromising, "unpoetic" subject, and has gone round and round it, disclosing the richness of its facets by means of some highly imaginative analogies. Whether these add up to a "définition-description" of the asparagus, or of just one man's responses to the asparagus, is another matter. The following lines from the opening of the poem exemplify much of what has been dealt with in this chapter, and illustrate the ambitions, the failures but also the achievements of Ponge:

Plus divisément encore que chez le cèdre, admiré-je peut-être chez l'asparagus cette façon de plafonner par chacun de ses hauts étages, de ne présenter au salut de la lumière (ou mettons à l'atterrissage en douce des avions de la lumière) que le dos de ses mains à hauteur de lèvres suspendues...chacune de ses branches est un long nuage effilé, un large nuage profilé—comme ceux qui s'étirent à l'horizon sur les plaines aux heures des crépuscules....

Merveilleusement arasés, ces hauts-tapis-volants-sur-place, planants, ces gazons maigres suspendus....

Strates en l'air....Ces tapis, ces tamis....

Flottilles de poissons plats à l'arrêt: soles, limandes, plies....

Flottilles de poissons squelettiques, fines charpentes faites des squelettes de ce genre de poissons, immobiles....

Even more evidently than in the cedar, I admire perhaps in the asparagus the way it has of reaching altitude through each of its high storeys, of only presenting to the salute of light (or shall we say to the soft landing of aeroplanes of light) the back of its hands at the height of hanging lips...each of its branches is a long frayed cloud, a wide streamlined cloud—like those which stretch out to the horizon over the plains at the sunset hour...

Marvellously even, these tall-flying-on-the-spot-carpets, planing, these thin suspended lawns....

Strata in the air....These carpets, these sieves....

Flotillas of flat fish come to a halt: sole, limanda, plaice....

Flotillas of skeletal fish, delicate frameworks made of the skeletons of this kind of fish, motionless...

(*N*, 133-34; Francis Ponge, *Nouveau Recueil*, Éditions Gallimard;
translated by Martin Sorrell)

CHAPTER 4

The Poems

THIS final chapter is devoted to the detailed analysis of a number of complete poetic texts by Ponge. They are chosen from five of his books; the aim is to present material which is representative of the major features of his creative work. For practical reasons, long texts cannot be included, all the more regrettable as some of the very longest—such as "La guêpe," "Le lézard," and "La chèvre" (this last named, fortunately, dealt with by Blossom Douthat)—are among Ponge's finest. It is not intended to say anything new about his theory and practice, rather to illustrate them. It seems worthwhile to devote space to this kind of practical criticism, given that Ponge is still relatively unfamiliar. Of course, as has been made clear in the foregoing chapters, there do already exist quite a number of analyses of individual texts of Ponge's, most of them valuable. As there has been a tendency among critics to concentrate on the same ones ("L'huître" seems to be a particular favorite), all but two of those selected in this chapter will, it is hoped, break new ground, and thus avoid pointless duplication. The exceptions are "Le gymnaste," about which Sartre has written, although not at length, and "La nouvelle araignée," which receives four pages in Lemichez's article "Origines inscrites."[1] The analytical approach in this chapter is orthodox. For more controversial, and semiological, interpretations, the reader is referred to the essays in *Francis Ponge: Colloque de Cerisy*, particularly to Jean-Michel Adam's examination of "Le lézard."

Trois poésies, III

Ces vieux toits
quatre fois
résignés

Ce hameau
sans fenêtres
sous les feuilles

C'est ton coeur
quatre fois
racorni

ta sagesse
hermétique
ô tortue!

These old roofs
four times
resigned

This hamlet
without windows
under the leaves

It's your heart
four times
hardened

your wisdom
hermetic
o tortoise!

(*T*, 15; Francis Ponge, *Tome premier*, Éditions Gallimard;
translated by Martin Sorrell)

One of Ponge's very earliest poems, "Trois poésies, III" was first published in 1926. In contradistinction to what he was to write later, it is composed along traditional lines. While the four stanzas do not have a clear rhyme pattern, each is three lines long, and each line has three syllables. The poem is obviously highly symmetrical, and its development carefully controlled.

The poem has no title; one feels that this omission is a deliberate part of the composition, for the last line, which is a revelation of what the previous eleven have been about, is both a climax and a belated title. "Ces vieux toits," it then becomes apparent, is the tortoise itself, more particularly the top section of its shell. Roofs for shells is a good metaphor, making the opening line striking as well as economical. The next two lines are more difficult; the meaning, arrived at on the basis of Ponge's predilection for elegant puns, seems to depend on the two possibilities of "résignés," "resigned" in the sense of "patient" and "accepting," and "re-signed," that is, bearing a number of signatures or physical marks. At least twice in *Méthodes* (88, 91), Ponge talks of signs in this way—the sign or signature on a pebble, and those he sees on a slate. So, in the present poem, Ponge is probably conveying that the tortoise by disposition is a patient, resigned animal, but also that its shell bears marks which can be considered its signature, that which gives it its particular character. A tortoise shell is in fact divided into more than four sections, so that the number four here may refer to something else. A possibility, given Ponge's technique of focusing on the act of creation within his creative pieces, is that "four" denotes the number of stanzas. The tortoise in this sense has four distinct physical marks made on its behalf by the poet.

The second stanza is more straightforward, again built around the good metaphor which makes up the first two lines. In the third stanza, the second line is a direct echo of the corresponding line of the first, though here it is not so easy to see why four in particular is the chosen number (except as a device imposed to provide echo). "Racorni" means "hardened," "with the hardness of horn," but, once more gaining depth through a pun, it can also denote a loss of mental agility and flexibility. Therefore, Ponge may be using this adjective to draw attention to the supposed mental slowness of the tortoise, suggested by its physical slowness, and, by association, to the animal's well-known ability to reach very old age.

However, if old age suggests dwindling intellectual strength, even senility, the last stanza of the poem shows that Ponge wants rather to evoke another aspect of old age, namely, wisdom. The move away from the suggestion of senility in the last line of the penultimate stanza is both a little surprising and effective, reinforced by the mysteriousness implicit in "hermétique." This short poem has used two good metaphors and two apt puns, it has suggested something old, slow, and patient, but has left the most enigmatic and intriguing feature in its correct place in the structure, the last stanza, before the declaration of the name "tortoise," a declaration possible only when the cumulative process has been finished. This withholding of the name, as we have seen, is quite typical of Ponge's method, and in this elegant and admirably structured little poem, the process is shown at its most convincing.

Les mûres

Aux buissons typographiques constitués par le poème sur une route qui ne mène hors des choses ni à l'esprit, certains fruits sont formés d'une agglomération de sphères qu'une goutte d'encre remplit.

Noirs, roses et kakis ensemble sur la grappe, ils offrent plutôt le spectacle d'une famille rogue à ses âges divers, qu'une tentation très vive à la cueillette. Vu la disproportion des pépins à la pulpe les oiseaux les apprécient peu, si peu de chose au fond leur reste quand du bec à l'anus ils en sont traversés.

Mais le poète au cours de sa promenade professionnelle, en prend de la graine à raison: "Ainsi donc," se dit-il, "réussissent en grand nombre les efforts patients d'une fleur très fragile quoique par un rébarbatif enchevêtrement de ronces défendue. Sans beaucoup d'autres qualités,— *mûres*, parfaitement elles sont mûres—comme aussi ce poème est fait."

On typographical hedgerows constituted by the poem on a route which does not lead out of things nor to the mind, certain fruits are formed of an agglomeration of spheres which a drop of ink fills.

Black, pink and khaki all at once on the cluster, they present more the spectacle of an arrogant family at its different ages than a very lively temptation to pick them. Given the disproportion between the pips and the pulp the birds enjoy them only a little, so little in the end remains with them when from beak to anus they are traversed by them.

But the poet in the course of his professional stroll learns from them a good lesson in the right measure: "Thus," he says to himself, "the patient efforts of a very fragile flower succeed in great numbers, although defended by a forbidding tangle of brambles. Without any other qualities—*ripe*, it is completely right to call blackberries ripe—just as this poem is complete."

(*T*, 41-42; Francis Ponge, *Tome premier*, Éditions Gallimard; translated by Martin Sorrell)

Here is one of Ponge's most tightly composed and successful examples of "adéquation." The first section in particular makes blackberries and printed words indissolubly a function of each other. The straight hedgerows, bearing black fruit full of dark juice are the lines on a page composed of black printer's ink, and vice versa.

The link which creates equivalence is the word "encre," which is to be taken simultaneously in a literal and metaphorical sense. The very first phrase indicates that the basis for the poem is going to be the metaphor-conceit of "poem-hedgerow." The first paragraph of the second section continues the figurative approach and seems a reasonably successful visual evocation of a patch of blackberries. The second paragraph of this section exemplifies Ponge's method of giving definition to an object in terms both of other things with which they have some association, but from which also they remain distinct. Here, it is birds, which feed on blackberries, on which blackberries rely to a certain extent for the dissemination of their seeds, but which at the same time do not enjoy the fruit, passing it with little trace through their bodies. It is as if the birds excrete to ensure that the blackberries remain discrete. In the second section, we find the familiar procedure in Ponge of defining things in terms of what they are not.

The second section reinforces the equivalence established in the first. A moral, almost allegorical, note is struck. The poet goes on a walk, physically beside blackberry patches, metaphorically along his poem. He sees blackberries, the black cluster of words on the page, as a metaphor of the act of writing; furthermore, they can provide him with a worthwhile example of the creative act while offering up to him their seeds (there is a play on "graine" and the expression "en prendre de la graine"). Patiently, a flower matures, both protected and, paradoxically, impeded by brambles ("défendue" can mean both "forbidden" and "protected"), suggesting the writer's struggle to create against all odds. The poem closes in a typical manner with the disclosure of the definitive word, "mûres." The fact that this word carries a pun makes the last sentence a conceit in which Ponge seals together the two aspects of the equivalence established at the outset. "Mûres" are blackberries, but the word is also the feminine plural of the adjective meaning "ripe." The time, therefore, when this fruit is ripe is the time when it finally deserves its name; it has reached its fulfillment, it is finished, and the moment of Ponge's saying so coincides with the finish, the fulfillment (the ripeness, therefore) of his poem. It can be seen that the words "mûres," "parfaitement," and "faits" in the last two lines are considerably loaded, and reveal the importance Ponge attaches to etymology.

Le gymnaste

Comme son G l'indique le gymnaste porte le bouc et la moustache que rejoint presque une grosse mèche en accroche-coeur sur un front bas.

Moulé dans un maillot qui fait deux plis sur l'aine il porte aussi, comme son Y, la queue à gauche.

Tous les coeurs il dévaste mais se doit d'être chaste et son juron est BASTE!

Plus rose que nature et moins adroit qu'un singe il bondit aux agrès saisi d'un zèle pur. Puis du chef de son corps pris dans la corde à noeuds il interroge l'air comme un ver de sa motte.

Pour finir il choit parfois des cintres comme une chenille, mais rebondit sur pieds, et c'est alors le parangon adulé de la bêtise humaine qui vous salue.

As his *G* indicates the gymnast sports a goatee beard and a moustache which a thick kiss-curl of hair on a low forehead almost touches.

In his tight-fitting costume which makes two folds on the groin, he also, like his *Y,* dresses on the left.

All hearts he devastates but owes it to himself to be chaste and his oath is ENOUGH!

More pink than is natural and less dexterous than a monkey he does his apparatus work with pure zeal. Then from the top of his body caught in the knotted rope he interrogates the air like a worm from its lump of earth.

To finish he drops sometimes from the rigging like a caterpillar, but bounces back on to his feet, and it is then the adulated paragon of human stupidity which salutes you.

(*T*, 72; Francis Ponge, *Tome premier*, Éditions Gallimard;
translated by Martin Sorrell)

This poem has received some comment from Sartre in his article in *Situations I*. While what he says is most valuable, his comments are deliberately selective and do not claim to have covered all the features in the poem. What Sartre points to is the way in which Ponge has turned a human being into an almost mechanical doll, certainly a largely dehumanized object.

The first line shows that the equivalence between gymnast (man) and "gymnast" (word) is calligrammatic. The letter *G* actually has the shape appropriate to the goatee beard and the falling curl of hair which Ponge sees as archetypal of gymnasts. This kind of preciosity (also in evidence, as has been mentioned already, in "La chèvre") is insistent here, for in the second paragraph, the letter *Y*, normally printed with heavier type in the left stroke and the down stroke, is taken to be an exact pictorial representation of the crotch of a male gymnast in his old-fashioned costume.

The third paragraph takes up the hint in "accroche-coeur" by casting the gymnast as something of a heart-throb. Ponge has chosen the verb "dévaster" in preference to, say, "briser," possibly for phonetic reasons. The "-aste" rhymes with "chaste" and "BASTE," and all three echo the subject of the poem, the gymn*ast*.

In the fourth paragraph, Ponge's technique of definition by differences is briefly evident. The gymnast not only is more pink than other men, but also he is said to be *not* a monkey. What Ponge has done, of course, is to put the idea of a monkey in our minds, reasonable in this context, and achieved a sort of simultaneous assertion and denial. To negate the monkey, he has to affirm it first. In the fine second sentence of this paragraph, there is an apt simile, humorous and ironical in the way it puts down the high-flying ambitions of the gymnast, and makes him as frail and insignificant as an earthworm. The simile presents a certain ambivalence. It could be taken to mean that the gymnast forms a question mark in the air ("interroge") in the same way that a worm's cast protrudes from the ground like a question mark. Or it might be, rather more literally, that the gymnast perched high up looks like a worm rising from its mound of earth. The early part of this sentence is what Sartre has in mind when he talks of the dehumanization of the gymnast. "Chef" for the more normal "tête" suggests that Ponge is moving away from the accepted denotations of humanity, something which is emphasized by the adjectival phrase "de son corps." The undercurrents of mechanism and behaviorism are particularly strong.

The final paragraph in fact makes these undercurrents deeper, and renders the poem as ironical as any in Ponge's work. First, the verb "choir," somewhat archaic, replaces the more predictable "tomber," and seems well suited to the fall of a caterpillar rather than that of a human being. The verb perfectly fits Ponge's second animal simile. The greatest irony is reserved for the very end. Ponge has put in opposition a word meaning "model of excellence" ("parangon") and another, typically one with two wholly appropriate senses, which means "stupidity" and, through its etymology, "animal condition" ("bêtise"). This latter gains added force by having, again ironically, the adjective "humaine" attached to it.

All in all, this is a poem which works well, perhaps because it avoids the risks of preciosity which it ran with the *G* and *Y* calligrams, and moves on instead to an acute observation of a particular human activity, almost an eccentricity, spiced with an irony which is none too cruel.

Flot

Flot, requiers pour ta marche un galet au sol terne
Qu'à vernir en ta source au premier pas tu perdes.

Wave, for your progress seek from the lusterless ground a pebble
Which to lose immediately on varnishing it in your spring.
                    (*T*, 138; Francis Ponge, *Tome premier*, Éditions Gallimard;
                                        translated by Martin Sorrell)

This shortest of Ponge's poems, dating from 1928, shows a compactness and density of structure and syntax suggestive of Mallarmé, though without his intellectual range and his sustained intricacy. The couplet seems to be an exercise in building with pairs of linked but opposed words. "Flot," the first word, may be seen as complemented by "galet," one suggesting flux, the other solidity. The imperative "requiers" opposes its idea of acquisition with that of loss in the last word of all, the verb "perdes" in the subjunctive, the mood indicating that the meaning is not "which you lose" so much as "in order to lose," or perhaps "with the result that you lose." "Marche" is linked, in the one example of union by similarity rather than by opposition, with "premier pas," both obviously denoting forward movement. "Sol," the element of earth, stands in relation to "source," the element of water. The adjective "terne" is paired with the following verb "vernir," where the polished effect of water removes the dullness of what might be either the ground or the pebble—it is possible that "terne" modifies "galet" or "sol," so that the meaning of the second part of the first line might be "a pebble on the dull ground," "a dull pebble on the ground," or even "a pebble which is dull when on the ground." Incidentally, the image of the dull pebble is one which Ponge had used earlier, in "Le galet" (*T*, 113), where the pebble is described as "terne au sol."

The aim of the poem seems to be to achieve a piece of writing that is near-perfect in its hermetically interlocking parts. The content is of no real substance, nor do the two lines illustrate the features and preoccupations, other than the quasi-Mallarmean search for a "necessary" language, by which Ponge is most recognizable. Nevertheless, "Flot" is a *tour de force* of linguistic precision.

Fable

> Par le mot *par* commence donc ce texte
> Dont la première ligne dit la vérité,
> Mais ce tain sous l'une et l'autre
> Peut-il être toléré?
> Cher lecteur déjà tu juges
> Là de nos difficultés....

> (APRÈS *sept ans de malheurs*
> *Elle brisa son miroir.*)

> By the word *by* this text then begins
> Whose first line tells the truth,
> But this silvering beneath the one and the other
> Can it be tolerated?
> Dear reader already you can judge
> From this our difficulties...

> (AFTER *seven years of misfortunes*
> *She broke her mirror.*)
> (*T*, 144; Francis Ponge, *Tome premier*, Éditions Gallimard;
> translated by Martin Sorrell)

Ponge indicates in the title that there is to be a moral, perhaps allegorical aspect to this "fable." Indeed, the bracketed postscript is an ironical reference to the superstition that if a person breaks a mirror, then seven years of bad luck will follow. A cryptic and reversed morality seems to be implied. While it is not openly stated, it is clear, especially in lines one and three, that the poem's subject is a mirror. The fact that the tone is one of difficulty, taken together with the postscript, may call to mind another superstitious belief, that mirrors and mirrorlike things are associated with danger as well as with images of truth.

Ponge may be trying to encompass danger and truth in this poem. The words "difficultés" and "vérité" are both used. He begins with a wordplay which is saved from being trivial by the fact that it renders the reflective effect of mirrors: "Par le mot *par* commence donc ce texte" not only offers perfect geometry in the first four words but, taken as a whole, is a model of self-reflection. This is capped by the second line whose purpose is to send us back to the first. In the third line, "tain," the "silvering" on mirrors, makes it clear that the poem's subject is a mirror, while the complete line is an example of near-calligrammatic "adéquation." "L'une et l'autre" must refer to the first two lines, which are therefore seen as the glass while the third line is exactly the underlying silvering which it says it is. This is reminiscent of the way Ponge found it appropriate to put his name underneath his text "Le pré." It is possible that in the fourth line, a play on "toléré" is intended. Apart from "allowed," it might mean "borne," signifying the physical act of lifting (the glass bearing the coat of silver, or conceivably vice versa). Nor may it be too fanciful to wonder if the word "tôle" was present in Ponge's mind. That word means "sheet-metal"; could Ponge be trying to suggest that it is difficult to give the silvering the solidity of metal which it would need to make the mirror last and function correctly?

By the end of the poem, the practical, and, allegorically, the poetic, difficulties have become such that the mirror cannot withstand them; the answer, presumably, to the question in line four is in the negative. "Fable," while of some curiosity, illustrates the trap of gratuitous obscurity into which Ponge occasionally falls when he tries for overclever effects.

Le nuage

Un linon humide et glacé flotte, dénoué du front qu'il sereina,
Où la transpiration a perlé....
Par mille étoiles.

Ainsi, lorsqu'il va fondre, bouge, et conçoit une molle chasse
Tout un bloc de cristaux plumeux.

A damp and frozen buckram floats, untied from the forehead which it
    serened,
Where perspiration has formed in beads.... Into a thousand stars.

So, when it is going to dissolve,
A whole block of feathery crystals
moves
and conceives a soft chase.

(*L*, 15; Francis Ponge, *Le Grand Recueil*, Vol. 1, Éditions Gallimard;
translated by Martin Sorrell)

A slight poem, in length as well as ambition, "Le nuage" nevertheless exhibits Ponge's ability to create striking imagery, and to join together elements in an effective conceit.

The poem opens with a metaphor; the cloud is seen as buckram, or lawn, a pleasing if undistinguished analogy, and the following adjectives are in no way adventurous. The second phrase of the first line, however, is more interesting. With a hint of preciosity, Ponge introduces personification—the "front" as the forehead of some deity perhaps, who is the sky—and then gives us the bolder stroke of an inverted verb in the past historic tense, "sereina." It is a happy coinage, for not only is the quality of serenity conveyed, appropriate to the "serene brow" of a crowned deity, but also "serein" as a noun means "precipitation of evening dew."

The second and third lines complete a conceit started in the first. "Sereina," in suggesting dew, and taken together with "front," leads into the fairly predictable image of beads of perspiration, in the second line. The third line then neatly unifies the different elements by means of the conceit of the drops of evening dew standing like beads of perspiration on the forehead of the sky.

Implicitly, the second stanza has changed the time of day; it is no longer nightfall. Ponge wants to convey now, through metaphor, exactly how it is when a cloud breaks up. To this end, he has used one or two slight but telling devices. First, he has put the idea of dissolving into the future ("va fondre"); the effect is to suggest a certain dramatic quality, also that the cloud itself is somehow destined to dissolve, that it is its mechanistic obligation to do so. Then, by means of an unusual word order, Ponge leaves to the end the naming of the most impressive feature, the visual metaphor that gives a high degree of focus to the dissolving cloud, namely, the feathery crystals. Ponge has inverted subject (all the last line) and two verbs, "bouge" and "conçoit," the latter accompanied by a direct object. The last aspect of Ponge's use of language to be noted in this poem, and which goes some way to achieving for it the status of "définition-description," is the juxtaposition of the noun "chasse" with an adjective which in strict terms should not belong to it, "molle." Obviously, it is transferred from "cristaux plumeux," but its modification of "chasse" seems to give added force to both noun and adjective.

Soir d'août

D'août le soleil du soir nous tisse des hamacs
A sa grosse patère au bat-flanc attachés;
Toboggans de soie blonde, métrages de tissu
Où rebondissent comme de vivantes miettes
Les moustiques dorés dont le bruit donne chaud.

Allongeons-nous, goûtons ces quarts d'heure de miel
Où dans le taffetas nos douleurs sont pansées.
L'or fauve est la couleur d'une gloire au déclin,
Sympathique déjà, d'où l'orgueil est banni,
Plus nourrissante et moins fermée sur soi.

. . . C'est ainsi que le soir nous accueille et nous choie,
Et vous convoque, horizontales joies.

Of August the evening sun weaves hammocks for us,
Which are attached to its thick dish with its swinging bail;
Toboggans of light-colored silk, lengths of material
On which bounce like living crumbs
The golden mosquitoes whose noise is warming.

Let us lie down, let us savor these honeyed quarter hours
Where in taffeta our pains are bandaged.
The fawn-tinted gold is the color of a declining glory,
Already pleasant, from which pride is banished,
More nourishing and less closed in on itself.

. . . It is thus that the evening welcomes us and molly-coddles us,
And calls you up, horizontal joys.
(*L*, 19; Francis Ponge, *Le Grand Recueil*, vol. 1, Éditions Gallimard;
translated by Martin Sorrell)

The traditional appearance of this poem makes it fairly unusual in Ponge's work, but nevertheless it is indicative of a certain respect he has for well-established prosody. The poem is in Alexandrines, except for the antepenultimate and the final lines. There is not what could be called a rhyme scheme, although of course the last three lines all do rhyme, reinforcing somewhat the traditional flavor of the piece.

The two large stanzas abound in analogy, used to conjure up a predominantly soft and soothing picture of an evening sky in summer. Typical of Ponge's use of metaphor, and to a lesser degree of simile, the comparisons are unusual, idiosyncratic, on occasions too far-fetched. The effects of light seen in terms of hammocks, with associations of relaxation and warmth, is a felicitous comparison, striking readier chords perhaps than the images contained in the awkward second line. Ponge indulges here his occasional taste for the overclever; "patère," meaning "patera," a dish used in classical times for libations or at sacrificial ceremonies, is not a common word by any means. It would be safe to assume that it evokes as little immediate response as "bat-flanc," the "swinging bail," or the piece of wood hung in a stable to keep horses separate from one another. The vocabulary in the second line is unfamiliar, the imagery does not appear to be appropriate.

Ponge looks to be on safer ground in the remainder of the first stanza. "Toboggans" is a bold metaphor, effectively conveying the notion of smooth lines, a wide visual sweep over which one can cast one's eye at speed. "Tissu," echoing "tisse," enhances the toboggan image, while the movement of the insects, caught in a conventional simile, completes a stanza which is basically one of orthodox poetic description.

Color and texture established in the first stanza carry over into the second ("miel," "taffetas," "l'or fauve"). Generally, this stanza poses fewer problems, is less difficult, although impressive in its evocation of the fading yet splendid light. The key word perhaps is "déclin." It is worth noting that the last two lines of this stanza give descriptive information about the evening sky by means of a "moral" content; that is to say, the color takes on the attributes of a sympathetic or agreeable nature in which there is no pride, and which is not closed, either physically or mentally.

The final couplet, again of a "moral" tendency, turns the attention away from the description and places it instead on the human. In this sense, perhaps, the poem is another of Ponge's fables. The evening is of ultimate significance for its effect on human behavior. Implicitly, human beings have the last word, for the "horizontal joys" is surely a coy, if not precious, way of referring to the pleasures of lovemaking at the end of the day. The poem thus ends tidily after moving from pure description to moral implications, the dominant tone of pleasure and tranquillity having been set in the very first word, with its pun on "doux," "soft."

14 juillet

Tout un peuple accourut écrire cette journée sur l'album de l'histoire, sur le ciel de Paris.

D'abord c'est une pique, puis un drapeau tendu par le vent de l'assaut (d'aucuns y voient une baïonnette), puis—parmi d'autres piques, deux fléaux, un râteau—sur les rayures verticales du pantalon des sans-culottes un bonnet en signe de joie jeté en l'air.

Tout un peuple au matin le soleil dans le dos. Et quelque chose en l'air à cela qui préside, quelque chose de neuf, d'un peu vain, de candide: c'est l'odeur du bois blanc du Faubourg Saint-Antoine,—et ce J a d'ailleurs la forme du rabot.

Le tout penche en avant dans l'écriture anglaise, mais à le prononcer ça commence comme Justice et finit comme ça y est, et ce ne sont pas au bout de leurs piques les têtes renfrognées de Launay et de Flesselles qui, à cette futaie de hautes lettres, à ce frémissant bois de peupliers à jamais remplaçant dans la mémoire des hommes les tours massives d'une prison, ôteront leur aspect joyeux.

A whole people hastening up to write this day into the album of history, on the Paris sky.

First it's a pike, then a flag stretched by the wind of the assault (some think it's a bayonet), then—among other pikes, two flails, one rake—on the vertical stripes of the sansculottes' trousers a cap thrown in the air as a sign of joy.

A whole people with the morning sun in their backs. And in the air something about it all which presides, something new, a little vain, candid: it's the smell of the white wood in the Faubourg Saint-Antoine—and that *J*, what's more, has the shape of a plane.

It all leans forward in its English written form, but when it's pronounced it begins like Justice and finishes la ça y est, and it's not the scowling heads of Launay and Flesselles, skewered on the ends of their pikes, which will take away their joyous aspect from this tall timber of letters, from this trembling poplar wood forever replacing in men's memories the massive towers of a prison.

(*Pi*, 50; Francis Ponge, *Le Grand Recueil*, vol. 3, Éditions Gallimard;
translated by Martin Sorrell)

The two principal features of interest in this poem, dated 1936, are the pride of place given to man as opposed to objects, and the possibilities for equivalence inherent in a letter of the alphabet.

The short introductory paragraph could in fact be considered the climax of the story, to which all the remainder of the poem is tending. Note that "accourut" is the only verb in a past tense, all the rest being in the present. It is of some importance, too, that the general activity of the crowd on the day the Bastille was stormed is assimilated to a creative act of writing.

The second paragraph reads like a catalog of objects associated with military and patriotic attitudes. "Fléau," as well as an agricultural flail,, denoted the similarly named old-fashioned and brutal instrument of war, while in a figurative sense it means "scourge," "pest," "curse." Ponge perhaps indulges in light irony in his reference to the trousers of the "sansculottes," literally "those without pants"; on the other hand, he is being exact, for this word was the name given, of course, in 1789 to the revolutionaries by the aristocrats when the former abandoned knee-length shorts in favor of the full-length trouser. The revolutionary "bonnet" is thrown into the air as a sign of joy, but perhaps also there is an echo of the phrase "jeter son bonnet par-dessus les moulins," an expression meaning "to behave badly, in defiance of good opinion." The phrase "signe de joie" takes us back to "écrire" in the first line; the revolutionaries are making the written signs of history by acting it out. More than that, however, the letter *J* is in a prominent position (as it is in the following "jeté"), and it may be to this that Ponge is referring at the end of the second paragraph. These *J*'s, and those in "juillet," "journée," "justice," and "joyeux" appear to be in positions of some importance in the context. What Ponge has done is to equate all the *J*'s, and then the words in which they appear, with feelings of joy, liberation, and revolution. In the first place, he sees the shape of the letter *J* as that of a plane (presumably upside down), used by the artisans of the Faubourg Saint-Antoine, an area of papermakers and of carpenters' shops.

In evoking this district of Paris, Ponge is alluding to the riot of 27 April 1789, in which revolutionaries, armed with long sticks (referred to in the last paragraph of the poem), were savagely put down by the Swiss Guard. As a plane, therefore, the letter *J* was in the service of revolution, and this equivalence is carried over into the final paragraph where *J* stands not only for Justice, but, being a tall letter, exactly represents the crude sticks the insurgents used against their oppressors. This new, tall, and defiant symbol will forever replace other kinds, such as the towers of the Bastille and other prisons, as well as the heads, perched on high poles, of Launay, the governor of the Bastille, and of the Provost Flesselles, both killed on the day the Bastille was taken. The reference at the beginning of the last paragraph to the English *J*, not pronounced the same way as in French, is not gratuitous. It is as if Ponge found the English pronunciation of "justice" more aggressive than the French, and therefore more in tune with its revolutionary emotions. Also, phonetically, English *J* (dze) permits an association with the phrase "ça y est," a slang expression meaning "this is it" or "here we go," perhaps meant to convey that, at the Saint-Antoine uprising, the Revolution had arrived, and with it, justice.

"14 juillet" is a poem which demonstrates certain features of Ponge's technique and, in a limited way, of his position as regards society. By choosing two violent and historically crucial days as his subject, he shows his own political leanings and demonstrates that man, often covertly but in this instance manifestly, can hold the center of his poetic stage.

La danseuse

Inaptitude au vol, gigots courts emplumés: tout ce qui rend une autruche gênée la danseuse toujours en pleine visibilité s'en fait gloire,—et marche sur des oeufs sur des airs empruntés.

D'âme égoïste en un corps éperdu, les choses à son avis tournent bien quand sa robe tourne en tulipe et tout le reste au désordre. Des ruisseaux chauds d'alcool ou de mercure rose d'un sobre et bas relief lui gravissent les temps, et gonflent sans issue. Elle s'arrête alors: au squelette immobile la jeune chair se rajuste aussitôt. Elle a pleine la bouche de cheveux qui s'en tireront doucement par la commissure des lèvres. Mais les yeux ne retinteront qu'après s'être vingt fois jetés aux bords adverses comme les grelots du capuchon des folies.

Idole jadis, prêtresse naguère, hélas! aujourd'hui un peu trop maniée la danseuse.... Que devient une étoile applaudie? Une ilote.

Inaptitude for flight, short and feathered legs of mutton: all that which makes an ostrich awkward the ballerina always in full view glories in it— and treads delicately with self-conscious airs.

Of an egotistical soul in a wild body, things according to her are turning out well when her dress turns tuliplike, and everything else turns into chaos. Hot streams of alcohol or of pink mercury of sober and low relief climb up her movements, and swell inescapably. Then she stops: to the motionless skeleton, the young flesh immediately readjusts itself. Her mouth is full of hair which will gently remove itself through the corner of the lips. But the eyes will ring out after having thrown themselves twenty times to the opposite edges like the little bells on a fool's cap.

Once an idol, formerly a priestess, alas! today a little too managed the ballerina. . . . What happens to a clapped and applauded star? A helot.

(*Pi*, 57; Francis Ponge, *Le Grand Recueil*, vol 3, Éditions Gallimard; translated by Martin Sorrell)

The harsh satire in this piece is at its most marked in the opening paragraph—in a way, a reversal of the process found in Renard's *Histoires naturelles*, where animals are treated with warmth and humor, and are appealing through the human characteristics bestowed on them. In Ponge's poem, the human being is made ridiculous, awkward, and off-putting by her resemblance to that most ungainly of animals, the ostrich. In addition, the first paragraph contains one of Ponge's cruellest analogies: the ballerina, symbol of feminine grace, is mutton with feathers stuck in it. She thinks that she turns to her own advantage all the most cumbersome aspects of the ostrich; the phrase "s'en fait gloire" suggests, however, Ponge's irony, even sarcasm, completed by "empruntés," meaning "affected" or "self-conscious." The girl's and the ostrich's movements are neatly linked by the idiom "marcher sur des oeufs," "to tread carefully," but literally, "to walk on eggs."

Ponge's habitual wordplay is in evidence in this poem, principally on two occasions in the second paragraph, and two in the third. The first word in the second is doubtless intended as a pun on "dame," while further in the sentence, Ponge literally makes his clauses turn on the verb "tourner," a wholly appropriate if predictable word in the context of a piece about a ballerina. The last word of the poem, which once denoted a slave or serf in ancient Sparta, is a near-reversal ("d——l," "l——t") of the paragraph's first word. To have two words whose meanings are virtually opposite and which reflect the transition from a high to a low position, is a simple yet effective device. The last wordplay of note is also in the last paragraph. "Maniée" would normally mean, applied to a professional performer or an artiste, "managed," "handled" by an impresario, etc. However, given the description, especially in the second paragraph, of a girl who is frenetic and disheveled, the noun "manie" also suggests itself, meaning "mania" or "derangement."

Ponge's brief surrealist connection may be recalled by two images in the second paragraph. The second and the last sentences both create images which could be interpreted as surrealistic, although they might rather be simply *recherché* and conventional, founded in rational association. The hot streams of alcohol and pink mercury are perhaps ways of describing the mixture of frenzy and a particular color apparent when the ballerina performs, but "gravissent les temps" is a juxtaposition which is bolder. There seems to be here some of the liberation of the imagination demanded by the surrealists, as there is in "les yeux. . . retinteront," in which sight has been directly linked with sound. The remainder of the sentence explains this juxtaposition; the bridge between sight and sound is "grelots," the little eye-shaped bells worn by that model of humor and seriousness, of frenzy and depth, the fool, the court jester.

Sartre's judgment that humans in Ponge's work are seen as objects is well borne out by "La danseuse." In this case, the result is not complimentary. The ballerina, while not a performing doll, by virtue of the considerable emotion and keyed-up energy with which she invests her dancing, is nevertheless an example of how human beings for Ponge are behavioristically determined, of how they are to be grasped, known, in terms of the routines which they perform. The ballerina is first and foremost a system of movements which she is obliged to execute, and which define her, in the same way as the gymnast in another poem. Even the young mother ("La jeune mère" in *Le Parti pris des choses*) is not so much an individual, distinguishable from all others, as a biological phenomenon who cannot help, like all young mothers, but act and react in the way she does. Ponge's aversion for lyricism is apparent not only in his use of language but also in his emotional response to his chosen subjects and objects.

L'appareil du téléphone

D'un socle portatif à semelle de feutre, selon cinq mètres de fils de trois sortes qui s'entortillent sans nuire au son, une crustace se décroche, qui gaîment bourdonne. . .tandis qu'entre les seins de quelque sirène sous roche, une cerise de métal vibre. . . .

Toute grotte subit l'invasion d'un rire, ses accès argentins, impérieux et mornes, qui comporte cet appareil.

(Autre)

Lorsqu'un petit rocher, lourd et noir, portant son homard en anicroche, s'établit dans une maison, celle-ci doit subir l'invasion d'un rire aux accès argentins, impérieux et mornes. Sans doute est-ce celui de la mignonne sirène dont les deux seins sont en même temps apparus dans un coin sombre du corridor, et qui produit son appel par la vibration entre les deux d'une petite cerise de nickel, y pendante.

Aussitôt, le homard frémit sur son socle. Il faut qu'on le décroche: il a quelque chose à dire, ou veut être rassuré par votre voix.

D'autres fois, la provocation vient de vous-même. Quand vous y tente le contraste sensuellement agréable entre la légèreté du combiné et la lourdeur du socle. Quel charme alors d'entendre, aussitôt la crustace détachée, le bourdonnement gai qui vous annonce prêtes au quelconque caprice de votre oreille les innombrables nervures électriques de toutes les villes du monde!

Il faut agir le cadran mobile, puis attendre, après avoir pris acte de la sonnerie impérieuse qui perfore votre patient, le fameux déclic qui vous délivre sa plainte, transformée aussitôt en cordiales ou cérémonieuses politesses.... Mais ici finit le prodige et commence une banale comédie.

From a portable cradle with a flat underlay, in accordance with five meters of flex of three kinds which intertwine without harming the sound, a crustacean unhooks itself, gaily humming...while between the breasts of some siren under a rock, a metal cherry vibrates....

All grottos suffer the invasion of a laughter, its silver-toned paroxysms, imperious and dull, which make up this instrument.

(Another)

When a little rock, heavy and black, bearing its lobster with difficulty, sets itself up in a house, the latter has to suffer the invasion of a laughter with silver-toned, imperious, and dull paroxysms. Doubtless it is the invasion of the sweet siren whose two breasts have appeared at the same time in a dark corner of the corridor, and which issues its call by the vibration between the two of a little nickel cherry, hanging there.

Immediately, the lobster trembles on its cradle. It has to be unhooked: it has something to say, or wants to be reassured by your voice.

At other times, the provocation comes from you yourself. When you are tempted into it by the sensually pleasant contrast between the lightness of the receiver and the heaviness of the cradle. What charm then to hear, as soon as the crustacean is unhooked, the gay hum which announces to you that the innumerable electrical vein-patterns of all the cities in the world are ready for any caprice of your ear!

You must turn the moveable dial, then wait, after having noted the imperious bell which perforates your patient, the well-known click which delivers you its complaint, transformed immediately into cordial or formal politenesses.... But here is where the wonder finishes and a banal comedy begins.

(*Pi*, 62-63; Francis Ponge, *Le Grand Recueil*, vol. 3, Éditions Gallimard; translated by Martin Sorrell)

The following analysis will be general, concentrating on the broad aesthetic issues the poem raises.

The two-part division of the poem demonstrates Ponge's practice of arriving at his definition-descriptions by means of accumulated detail, much of it repeated in slightly modified forms. Here, largely the same vocabulary is used in different combinations. It can be seen that the primary images center on the crustacean (incidentally, Ponge has replaced the noun "crustacé" with his own invention "crustace," for reasons which are not clear), in particular the lobster, and related sirens, caves, and grottos. He is not afraid to mix his images, however, and he does so without causing confusion or missing his effects. His overall metaphors are not mixed. Rather, Ponge keeps his different categories of images, metaphors, etc. quite separate as a rule; a good example of this is the whole of the second section. The telephone is first seen as a siren; the two bells, presumably fixed to a wall in another part of the house, are seen as the siren's breasts; the bell-hammer between them, a cherry.

The reader who knows Ponge's work well will be familiar with this technique, which can be seen both as part of his use of the analogical mode, and also, more arguably, perhaps, as an aspect of the wish to define things discretely. That is to say, Ponge's metaphors and similes, even when, as in this instance, they act conjunctively by likening the object to other objects, nevertheless recognize the autonomy of all things. There is a case for claiming that when Ponge piles up disparate metaphors, searching for more and more ways of getting to the essence of an object, arriving at his cumulative definitions, these metaphors are acting more as similes. By not sustaining one particular metaphor, but constantly changing their type and their associations (their "resonance," to use one of Ponge's own terms), he seems to maintain his distance from them, and a certain doubt about them. His telephone, or bell, or hammer remain just these things; and lobsters, breasts, and cherries are kept at arm's length, despite appearance, and stay as speculations about the former, their correlates. Recalling what was said in the last chapter, Ponge's use in this poem of metaphors suggests that he is taking a relativist position about the telephone, believing that this appliance is a number of other things too, that its reality is not fixed. On the other hand, the strong suggestion of simile (assuming that the reader agrees that this is in fact a correct reading of the poem) would make Ponge's view of the telephone absolutist, on the basis that while it is like several things, it remains fixedly apart from those things.

This poem raises one or two other broad issues in Ponge's poetics. Possibly more than any of the other texts examined so far in this chapter, it can be considered an example of the "objeu," certainly of the "objoie," and of the "en abîme" technique. The most banal of objects has been selected for intense scrutiny, and by opening up language largely through the resources of analogy (though admittedly with little if any of the etymological precision found elsewhere), Ponge has been able to render the richness and variety of an object at which nobody would normally ever look closely, and to recreate it as "objoie." The sharp focus which makes the telephone seem twice as large and significant as usual can be seen as the process of putting it right at the center of consciousness, "en abîme."

All of this, in terms not used by Ponge himself, calls to mind phenomenology's eidetic reduction. The telephone has been lifted out of its habitual context and has become the object of the total attention of consciousness. Tinged with humor as this "définition-description" is, it might be seen as a less morbid counterpart of Roquentin's X-raying of the chestnut tree and of the tram-seat in Sartre's *La Nausée*. In both cases, whether it is in terms of viscous messes and centipedes for Sartre or crustacea and cherries for Ponge, objects are shown with intensity to be what appears to consciousness.

This in turn raises the problem of essence. In *La Nausée*, part of the intention of the phenomenological mode of perception is to tell us something about a fictional character. In "L'appareil du téléphone," not only is there no such fictional character to whom the choice of perceptions may be attributed, but Ponge's aesthetic, as has been seen, involves the notion that things can be their own spokesman, that it is their consciousness which is being displayed. We are therefore faced with the task of reconciling the fact that images and metaphors have been created by Ponge and the wish he has of making us believe that these same images and metaphors emanate from the objects themselves. If Ponge has achieved eidetic reduction in this poem, and come some of the way toward revealing the "truth," or "truths," about the telephone, he has had to do so by replacing its commonly recognized context and accretions with others of his own. To look at it afresh, in its starkness, has in fact meant providing a new and personal context and set of associations. Again, therefore, we are confronted with the problem that to *say* anything which aspires to definition and description, the user of language is forced to have recourse to analogy, which necessarily tells as much if not more about the user as about the thing. In this poem, Ponge's images are elaborate, even somewhat baroque in their extravagance, whereas a telephone could be thought of as sober, worthy of the most restrained and colorless metaphors. The poem speaks about Ponge's telephone, not The Telephone. If a writer starts using metaphor for such a definitive-descriptive task, then the inescapable conclusion is that there are many other possible metaphors which could be created, doubtless equally aptly, by other writers.

Le gui

Le gui la glu: sorte de mimosa nordique, de mimosa des brouillards. C'est une plante d'eau, d'eau atmosphérique.
Feuilles en pales d'hélice et fruits en perles gluantes.
Tapioca gonflant dans la brume. Colle d'amidon. Grumeaux.
Végétal amphibie.
Algues flottant au niveau des écharpes de brume, des traînées de brouillard,
Épaves restant accrochées aux branches des arbres, à l'étiage des brouillards de décembre.

Mistletoe bird lime: sort of northern mimosa, mimosa of the fogs. It is a water plant, atmospheric water.
Propellor-blade leaves and sticky-pearl fruit.
Tapioca swelling in the mist. Starch paste. Curds.
Amphibious plant life.
Seaweed floating at the level of the scarves of mist, of the trails of fog,
Flotsam remaining caught in the branches of the trees, at the low-level mark of the December fogs.

(*Pi*, 65; Francis Ponge, *Le Grand Recueil*, vol. 3, Éditions Gallimard;
translated by Martin Sorrell)

Written in 1941, a year before the publication of *Le Parti pris des choses*, this poem could just as well be part of that collection as of *Pièces*. It is typical of the shorter poems, arguably better represented in *Pièces* than in *Le Parti pris des choses*, which condense uniform information and images into a single concentrated "définition-description" which is, literally, monotonous. Where "L'appareil du téléphone" was variegated, disparate, and baroque, "Le gui" is monochrome, unified, and classical in a certain sense.

Images are grouped around the color white, but an insipid, watery off-white. Bird lime, mist, and fog, tapioca, paste, curds, all are associated with this color, while the texture of mistletoe, somewhere between the liquid and the viscous, is strongly brought out by the evocation of lime, water, glue, seaweed. "Glu" is principally obtained from the holly tree; it also has the meaning of a "lure," a "temptation." Ponge thus begins his poem (using the simplest device of juxtaposing two nouns), by establishing three levels of association: mistletoe is sticky and viscous, it is inviting, personally attractive to Ponge (and by extension to other people as well), and it evokes Christmas, season of these two trees. The opening phrase of "Le gui" is an example, admittedly an undeveloped one, of one of the qualities of the "objeu," the internal multiplication of the relationships of words. Other features of the "objeu" are also demonstrated. The "rigorous harmony of the world" which Ponge associates with the "objeu" may be seen in his use of analogies. In a particularly elliptical fashion (phrases, individual words, are simply listed without being integrated into clauses or sentences), Ponge brings together things which, while discrete, are much more closely associated with one another than is normal in his work. Tapioca, paste, curds, are convincing metaphors for mistletoe's texture, as mimosa, propellor-blades and pearls (or beads) for its look. Instead of definition by differences, we find here definition by similarity and near-homogeneity. The world, disclosed as off-white and viscous, seems indeed harmonious.

A successful, compact, and unified poem, "Le gui" perhaps indicates not only that Ponge is a master of a particular kind of evocation of material things, but that he is at times quite close to other poets; for Rimbaud surely achieved a comparable result in his "Sonnet des voyelles," this also a poem on the equivalents in language for certain colors.

La nouvelle araignée

Au lieu de tuer tous les Caraïbes, il fallait peut-être les séduire par des spectacles, des funambules, des tours de gibecière et de la musique.

(VOLTAIRE.)

Dès le lever du jour il est sensible en France—bien que cela se trame dans les coins—et merveilleusement confus dans le langage, que l'araignée avec sa toile ne fasse qu'un.

Si bien—lorsque pâlit l'étoile du silence dans nos petits préaux comme sur nos buissons—

Que la moindre rosée, en parole distinctes,
Peut nous le rendre étincelant.

Cet animal qui, dans le vide, comme une ancre de navire se largue
d'abord,
  Pour s'y—voire à l'envers—maintenir tout de suite
  —Suspendu sans contexte à ses propres décisions—
  Dans l'expectative à son propre endroit,
  —Comme il ne dispose pourtant d'aucun employé à son bord, lorsqu'il
veut remonter doit ravaler son filin:
  Pianotant sans succès au-dessus de l'abîme,
  C'est dès qu'il a compris devoir agir autrement.

  Pour légère que soit la bête, elle ne vole en effet,
  Et ne se connaît pas brigande plus terrestre, déterminée pourtant à ne
courir qu'aux cieux.
  Il lui faut donc grimper dans les charpentes, pour—aussi aériennement
qu'elle le peut—y tendre ses enchevêtrements, dresser ses barrages, comme
un bandit par chemins.

  Rayonnant, elle file et tisse, mais nullement ne brode,
  Se précipitant au plus court;
  Et sans doute doit-elle proportionner son ouvrage à la vitesse de sa
course comme au poids de son corps,
  Pour pouvoir s'y rendre en un point quelconque dans un délai toujours
inférieur à celui qu'emploie le gibier le plus vibrant, doué de l'agitation la
plus sensationnelle, pour se dépêtrer de ces rets:
  C'est ce qu'on nomme le rayon d'action,
  Que chacune connaît d'instinct.

  Selon les cas et les espèces—et la puissance d'ailleurs du vent—,
  Il en résulte:
  Soit de fines voilures verticales, sorte de brise-bise fort tendus,
  Soit des voilettes d'automobilistes comme au temps héroïques du sport,
  Soit des toilettes de brocanteurs,
  Soit encore des hamacs ou linceuls assez pareils à ceux des mises au
tombeau classiques.

  Là-dessus elle agit en funambule funeste:
  Seule d'ailleurs, il faut le dire, à nouer en une ces deux notions,
  Dont la première sort de corde tandis que l'autre, évoquant les
funérailles, signifie souillé par la mort.

  Dans la mémoire sensible tout se confond.
  Et cela est bien,

Car enfin, qu'est-ce que l'araignée? Sinon l'entéléchie, l'âme immédiate,
commune à la bobine, au fil, à la toile,
    A la chasseresse et à son linceul.

Pourtant, la mémoire sensible est aussi cause de la raison,
Et c'est ainsi que, de *funus* à *funis*,
Il faut remonter,
A partir de cet amalgame,
Jusqu'à la cause première.

Mais une raison qui ne lâcherait pas en route le sensible,
Ne serait-ce pas cela, la poésie:

Une sorte de *syl-lab-logisme?*
Résumons-nous.

L'araignée, constamment à sa toilette
Assassine et funèbre,
La fait dans les coins;
Ne la quittant que la nuit,
Pour des promenades,
Afin de se dégourdir les jambes.

Morte, en effet, c'est quand elle a les jambes ployées et ne ressemble plus
qu'à un filet à provisions,
    Un sac à malices jeté au rebut.

Hélas! Que ferions-nous de l'ombre d'une étoile,
Quand l'étoile elle-même a plié les genoux?

La réponse est muette,
La décision muette:

(L'araignée alors se balaye....)

Tandis qu'au ciel obscur monte la même étoile—qui nous conduit au jour.

Instead of killing all the Caribs, it might have been better to win them
over with shows, tight-rope walkers, conjuring tricks and music.

(VOLTAIRE)

From daybreak it is apparent in France—although the plot is being woven in corners—and marvellously confused in language, that the spider and its web make one.

So much so that—when the star of silence grows pale in our little yards as on our hedges—
The least hint of dew, in distinct words,
Can make it sparkle for us.

This animal which, like a ship's anchor, first casts off into the open,
And straightaway—granted, upside down—holds itself there
—Suspended out of context from its own decisions—
In expectation of its rightful place,
—As it does not have helpers on board it is forced to swallow its thread again when it wants to climb back up:
Strumming its failure above the abyss,
It grasps finally that it must try another line.

Light though the beast is, it certainly does not fly,
And will not recognize that there is no more earthbound brigand, determined instead to run around the heavens.
So it has to climb up in the rafters, to—as airily as possible—spread out its entanglements, erect its barriers, like a highwayman.

Radiating, it spins and weaves, but on no account embroiders,
Going the shortest way;
And without doubt it has to adjust its amount of work to the speed of its travel, as to its body weight,
To be able to get to any given point always in less time than is the case with the most thrashing prey, given the most sensational contortions, to disentangle itself from those nets:
This is what is called the range of action,
Which all spiders know instinctively.

Depending on the situation and the species—and on top of that the strength of the wind—
The result is:
Either a fine vertical spread of sails, a kind of very taut window-curtain,
Or motorists' veils as in the heroic early days of the sport,
Or the dresses in junk shops,
Or even hammocks or shrouds rather like those used in classic entombments.

Thereupon, it does its funereal funambulist's routine:
Alone, as a matter of fact, in being able to tie together these two notions,
The first of which, evoking obsequies, signifies sullied by death, while the second stems from the word for rope.

In a retentive memory all is mixed up.
Which is a good thing.
For in the end what is the spider? If not the entelechy, the very centre
strand, common to spool, thread and web,
To the huntress and her shroud.

And yet, the retentive memory is also the cause of reasoning,
And so, from *funus* to *funis*,
It is necessary to go back up,
From this amalgam,
Until you reach the first cause.

But a reasoning which would not suddenly leave go halfway through of
the retentive intelligence,
Isn't that what poetry is:

A sort of *syl-lab-logism?*
Let's sum up so far.

The spider constantly at its
Murderous and funereal toilette,
Does it in corners;
Stopping only at night-time,
To go for constitutionals,
To stretch its legs.

It is dead indeed when its legs are curled in and looks like nothing more
than a string shopping-bag,
A bag of malice tossed out.

Alas! What should we do with the shadow of a star,
When the star itself has crumpled at the knees?

The reply is silent,
The decision silent:

(The spider can then be swept out. . . .),

While in the dark sky the same star rises—and leads us toward day.
(*Pi*, 197-200; Francis Ponge, *Le Grand Recueil*, vol. 3, Éditions Gallimard;
                                       translated by Martin Sorrell)

This second of two texts about the spider (the first, "L'araignée,"
is also included in *Pièces*) is one of Ponge's best known poems, has

appeared in anthology, and has been translated at least twice.[2] Such prominence can easily be explained, for "La nouvelle araignée" brings together, as successfully as in any other text, a large number of the important features of Ponge's poetics, and, despite its length, remains well structured and excellently balanced.

It is both a "définition-description" of the spider and a poem about poetry. This second aspect, which becomes totally disclosed by the end, is implicit in the first sentence. Just as spider and its web are one, the former weaving the latter, so a parallel act of fabrication is being performed out of the "confusion" (blend as well as muddle) of language. The unity of spider and web is brought out by the dew, either gifted with powers of expression or, as put forward in Ponge's poetics, relying on man's ability to be expressive on its behalf. The last four lines of the first section, therefore, seem to be saying that when the spider fades like a star (or dies, for this image ties up with the last few lines of the poem), it can be reborn in a language created both by the dew and by the poet. Ponge implies that the spider, like the star, comes out at night and by contrast is dead, metaphorically or literally, by day. One becomes aware of the results of its activity when, at daybreak, one finds completed webs. The first section of the poem establishes a cycle, based on the image of the star, of rising and falling, of light and dark, of night giving way to dawn. The cycle is rounded off in the last line of all, where the death of one spider is only followed by the birth, and the literal rise, of another.

Having set out the crucial metaphor of the star, a conceit through its range of rather recondite associations—one of which is the play allowed by "étoile" on "toile," meaning "spider's web"—Ponge launches into one of his best-sustained looks at a single object. Many features of his method encountered in the previous chapters are in evidence. Similes, metaphors obviously, puns, and wordplay of a sort which seems more serious in that it aims to reach a simultaneous truth both about the word and the thing to which it applies. The examples are copious; one need pick out only a few. In the second section, "filin," meaning "rope," is a good choice for the spider's thread, as it suggests "fil." Then, in the first line of the third section (in which, incidentally, as in the first line of the fourth section, there is an example of definition by negation), there is a pun on "vole," meaning both "to fly" and "to steal," a possibility then developed by the nouns "brigande" and "bandit." "Rayonnant" and "rayon" in the fourth section are carefully used; they carry the various meanings of "radius," thereby suggesting the circularity of the web, of "ray of light," recalling the final word of the first section, and of the "points of a star," which leads back to the central image of the poem.

The fifth section is a series of metaphors, imaginative and convincing. It is interesting that if these metaphors do not really exemplify "adéquation," but tell us more about Ponge's fertile views of the spider rather than about the spider's own view of itself, Ponge has achieved "adéquation" of sorts by the play on "soit," suggesting "soie," a word not infrequently used to describe a web. Again, with "toilettes," Ponge has happily hit upon a word which serves him well, as of course it could be seen as a diminutive of "toile."

In the following section, Ponge makes clear that etymologies are a cornerstone of his poetics, and his interpretation of "funeste" and "funambule" demonstrates the way in which he makes words and objects necessarily, not arbitrarily, interdependent. Furthermore, he does not so much bring together the notions of "funereal" and "funambulist," he "ties" them ("nouer"), a verb obviously suggestive of rope and thread. On the matter of these two words, in the eighth section, Ponge gives "remonter" both of its meanings, literally "to go up," as the spider goes up its thread, and "to trace back," of etymologies. On occasions, his wordplay can be more subtle. "Ame" (section seven), linked to "entéléchie" by their shared meaning of "soul" or "essence," has the comparatively rare secondary meaning of "core" or "central strand" of a rope. This is precisely the correct and fully *adequate* use of language which Ponge endlessly postulates in his theoretical writings.

However, ingenuity can spill over into inaccuracy. Doubtless the major reason for using the rare "entéléchie" is that its root, Greek "talos," very much resembles the root of "toile," Latin "tela." The link, therefore, is one of suggestion and no more. Yet the apposition is effective for another possible reason; an aspect of the meaning of "entelechy" is "the force by which an object passes from one state to a second state," and in this way the word is appropriate to the picture of the spider spinning itself into its fully evolved state. There is one more possibility as well; "entelechy," combining its secondary meaning of "essence" with that of "containing perfection," may be seen as the principle underlying the pattern in which the central energy (spider, spool, etc.) is surrounded by webs and threads, always traceable back to the center, the core.

The most marked piece of wordplay, however, is the coining in the tenth section, "syl-lab-logisme." Not an elegant word, it conveys the idea of "syllable," of "syllogism," and of "logic," all of which have relevance to the poem. But, arguably, this single word is the most glaring example of preciosity in this piece. By implying a logical basis in poetry, Ponge calls to mind his dictum about "réson-raison"; indeed, he used "raison" in section nine. In terms of the structure of "La nouvelle araignée," the introduction of this matter at this stage coincides with the opening out of the poem; Ponge has finished the main descriptive part, and he turns to the question, present from the opening lines, of poetry itself. As is normal in his work, he does not enter into a discussion of poetics which is rigorous or even informative. Instead, his aim is to keep in the forefront of his and our consciousnesses the fact that objects and poems are so necessary to each other that, while they do not become indistinguishable, we are almost made to ask, according to Richard[3], if the poem is a function of the object, or the object a function of the poem. Ponge's poetics do seem to lead to this position, and if one accepts that this is in fact his principal aim, again it is striking how crucial is the matter of equivalence.

To return to the poem's structure, sections nine and ten, as well as firmly establishing this work as a poem about poems, act as a transition to the final part, beginning with the "résumé" in section eleven. It has been seen previously how Ponge composes cumulatively, repeating words and phrases, shifting emphases, refusing to discard as he goes along language he has tried thus far. Hence the often-felt effect that his texts are a compilation of notes, of "notes toward" the definitive text. This is all part of the process of moving round and round the object, getting new perspectives and new toeholds. Clearly, by section eleven, Ponge feels that he is moving toward a definition of the spider, and that the end of his poem is in sight. So, instead of leaving it after this section, he makes the end, with equivalence probably in mind, coincide with the end of the object. From the twelfth to the penultimate section, the tone is one of death. Of course, this is not unprepared, and part of this poem's strength is that it is closely argued and perfectly unified. From the metaphor of burial shrouds (section five) onward, the spider is seen as a black associate of death. The last sections provide some splendid metaphors, until, in the line in parenthesis, the spider, once a star, now a mere shadow, has been reduced to nothing more than an inconvenience. Here, perhaps, is evidence of Ponge's humor, or irony. He is the champion of dumb ("muette," section fourteen) things, his "parti pris" is for them, and so, as happens in this poem, a trivial or even a unpleasant object is momentarily aggrandized. Yet, the effect of the last sections seems to be to put everything back into its accepted order. It looks as though, after all, Ponge subscribes to the unthinking attitudes of other men, and that he has fallen back into the complacency of the "vieil humanisme." We might think that he is gently chiding himself for having become so serious about something so unnoteworthy. Indeed, the suggestion in section four of a measure of mechanistic harmony—the correct proportions in the spider's makeup, its instinctive behavior—could cause Ponge to feel satisfied with the order of things, a comfortable order with man still at the center.

However, the last line of all is masterly. The illusion of an anthropocentric world in which spiders (magnified, incidentally, into beasts earlier in the poem) are to be brushed away, shriveled and compact in death, is neatly destroyed. In the constant cycle of night and day, the same star, but constituted by a *new* spider—the explanation of the poem's title comes at the very end—will rise inexorably, by implication as durable as man, and will continue the cycle of time by ushering in day, which is the point at which we came in at the beginning of the poem. The cycle is complete, it is also endless, and in terms of the poem's other level of meaning, "jour" may be seen as a metaphor of the text itself; that ever-rising star, the spider, will send the poet back to the living, creative act of rendering it in language.

In this important poem, Ponge has achieved a number of things, the central one of which, perhaps, is to suggest not only that the spider and the web are bound together literally, but that, figuratively, the poet also binds them together by his weaving of linguistic webs. "La nouvelle araignée" is a major example in Ponge's work of what he means by "natural secretion," an idea of great significance in his aesthetics. As the snail cannot help but secrete slime, or the mollusc its own shell, so the spider must secrete its web. These are mechanistic obligations matched by man's compulsion to give out his own "true secretion," language.

CHAPTER 5

Conclusion

P ONGE is an uneven and sometimes contradictory writer. His pronouncements on matters of poetic theory and practice are generally of interest, limited perhaps, and marred all too often by needless repetition and by an annoying current of exaggerated self-importance. It is fair to say that certain critics have been much more illuminating about his work than he ever has himself.

By contrast, some of Ponge's poems—though not all, for his uneven quality extends to his creative as well as to his theoretical writings—are extremely impressive, and it seems to be reasonably safe to conjecture that Ponge will be remembered for such little gems as "Le pain," "Le papillon," and "Le gymnaste" long after his theoretical pieces have been forgotten. Even such texts as *La Fabrique du Pré* and *Comment une figue de paroles et pourquoi* demonstrate that the point of real impact is more the finished poem than the various ways used to get to it.

The broad picture which emerges from all Ponge's poems and poetics is, composed around the central philosophical and technical issue of equivalence ("adéquation"), an apparently new kind of poetic world which has tried to accommodate certain problems about what language is, how it functions, and how it can be made to be more than the mirror for what Ponge sees as man's narcissism. The way out of this "magma," this "manège," is by a reformulation of the laws of linguistic (not syntactical, incidentally) practice which in turn can only come about when men cease to think and to see anthropomorphically, and instead reinstate the nonhuman world. This desire of Ponge's may in the end be seen as mystical, although his mysticism is firmly nontranscendental. Ponge does not seek to interpret the world; that he aims to do nothing other than reveal it, as it is, is crucial. Thus, it is not profitable to try to decide whether the phenomenal world according to Ponge is grammatical or absurd; at various points in his work, there is evidence for both contentions. The world is often but not always seen as mechanistic, behavioristic, therefore, by implication, harmonious. Like a phenomenologist, Ponge adopts the method of staring as hard as possible at the world, aiming to disclose its solid presence, uncontaminated by the distorting attitudes of mind which men normally interpose between themselves and it.

But in this lies the difficulty. It is one thing to stand back from the world and to make philosophically and religiously neutral statements about it.[1] It is another to claim that a new use of language will tip the balance in favor of things and against man, and allow them to speak for themselves, independently of him. The main problem, then, which arises from the central issue in Ponge's work is simply that man will not go away on those occasions when Ponge might like him to. Ponge is of course not so naïve as to have believed otherwise; at least, the gist of his remarks about "relative" and "absolute" successes in linguistic and poetic enterprises, his settling for the former when his inclination might have been to the latter, indicate that he recognizes the truth (revealed in phenomenology) that a statement made about the world is in part a statement about the perception of it. A human perceiver is posited. Because of this, perhaps, Ponge's poems do not amount to ontological statements, although there would seem to be an ontological aim in having the world disclose itself as it really is, which contrasts with Ponge's acceptance that his success in facilitating this disclosure can only be a relative one.

For the revelation of the truth of the world, of its animate and inanimate nonhuman components, an "absolute" language is necessary. Ponge concedes that he cannot establish this, yet he has favored certain techniques—notably, etymological precision and depth, and variations on the same phrases—which would lead him some way in the right direction. Ponge's ambition resembles Mallarmé's, though it is less rigorous, less syntactically shut in. It is as if Ponge shared Mallarmé's aspiration to make language partake of the quality of music, that is, words should be made absolutes and not approximations. But whereas Mallarmé wanted a kind of self-referring language, Ponge's aim, somewhat different, would be to have a language which referred to its correlates in the world in an absolutely necessary way. His poems would therefore not be about a pebble, but about The Pebble; not about a suitcase, but about The Suitcase; not about a horse, but about The Horse. That many critics and readers feel that Ponge's poems, whatever their merits, have not achieved this indicates that the ambition to create an absolute language has not been realized. It might be added that the same conclusion can be reached about Mallarmé.

The problem of anthropomorphism persists, therefore. Not only does a perception of the world and its objects presuppose a human perceiver, partial and selective, but his rendering of that perception calls upon the services of a man-made, "relative" commodity, language. Ponge is of course alive to this possibly ironical fact. Indeed, he turns it to his own advantage by invoking humanism. He says that the poet should push himself to write things that are difficult, to aim high, for the careful, implicitly the poetic, use of language is a manifestation of heroism, of a heroic humanism (*T*, 217). It is worth mentioning that in the same paragraph, Ponge talks of this activity in terms of the attempt man must make to express himself. Part of Ponge's complexity is that, despite his persistent "parti pris" in favor of things, he never loses sight of man's responsibility, his direct involvement, in the setting up of these things' autonomy. In fact, he brings together the two strands of his thinking, the thing-centered and the man-centered, by establishing a mechanistic, behavioristic model of the world in which man has no option but to produce language as the snail secretes its shell, trees form leaves, or water flows to the lowest possible level. Sartre has tidily summed up and joined together these behavioristic and humanist attitudes: "Ponge est humaniste. Puisque parler, c'est être homme, il parle pour servir l'humain en parlant."[2]

It is difficult to situate Ponge within any particular tradition in French poetry. In some ways, he is a Mallarmean, but he also frequented the surrealists. Despite his political convictions, he never becomes a political poet in the way that, say, Aragon did. His resolute antilyricism makes him part company with a host of other poets, as does of course his particular and idiosyncratic techniques as well as his choice of subject matter and attitudes towards it. In limited ways, he might be compared to Guillevic and Follain. It is tempting, but probably misleading, to link him with the scientific current in literature during the Renaissance and with nineteenth-century positivism. But, as Robbe-Grillet points out,[3] Ponge's poetry is not truly based in science, just as it is not exactly descriptive.

If anything, Ponge suggests, not too insistently, what Jules Renard might have done with his excellent *Histoires naturelles* if he had had more philosophical and didactic tendencies. The comparison between Ponge and Renard is intended to be only very speculative. So, too, is the tentative comparison between Ponge and

Gerard Manley Hopkins, whose "inscape"—the definition he offers of the interior landscape of things—may be said to resemble Ponge's own concern with a definitive "inner" truth of things. What must be said in conclusion is that Ponge, when at his best, notably in *Le Parti pris des choses* and *Pièces*, has written poems which, novel in aspect but so often quite traditional in their respect for certain time-honored conventions of poetic craftsmanship, their reliance above all on analogical modes, are nevertheless unique, unlike anything else in French poetry, and of a very high order. Often, he has come close to his goal of making his poem and the object it is describing functions of each other. So much are the two fused together in some cases that we are hard put to decide whether the word signifies the object, or the object the word. Surely without doubt, the poems and texts in Ponge's uneven output which most fully and successfully approximate to his own dictum about the desired "définition-description-oeuvre d'art littéraire," with all its implications about precise observation, linguistic care and sophistication, and respect for the codes of artistic practice, are those which have secured and will maintain Ponge's reputation.

Notes and References

Chapter One

1. *Entretiens de Francis Ponge avec Philippe Sollers* (Paris, 1970), p. 41.
2. Quoted in Philippe Sollers, *Francis Ponge* (Paris, 1963), p. 64.
3. Jean Thibaudeau, *Ponge* (Paris, 1967), p. 29.
4. Ibid., p. 54.
5. *Entretiens*, p. 65.
6. Ibid., p. 68.
7. Sollers, p. 74.
8. Ponge, *Tome premier* (Paris, 1965), p. 74; hereafter cited in the text as *T*.
9. Ibid., p. 126.
10. See also *Méthodes* (vol. 2 of *Le Grand Recueil* [Paris, 1961]), p. 224, where Ponge says that the world, including men, is "écriture *non significative.*" *Méthodes* is hereafter cited in the text as *M*.
11. These comments on phenomenology and the new novel largely derive from the excellent exposition given by J. Sturrock in his *The French New Novel* (London, 1969).
12. Page references to *Tome premier, Nouveau Recueil*, and *Méthodes* will not normally indicate from which particular collection, essay, or section within these three volumes the extracts are taken. *Nouveau Recueil* is hereafter cited in the text as *N*.
13. See *Méthodes*, p. 14: "Ce que je tenterai sera donc de l'ordre de la définition-description-oeuvre d'art littéraire." It is clear that much more than mere description is envisaged.
14. *Tome premier*, p. 308.

Chapter Two

1. *Méthodes*, p. 9.
2. See *Pour un Malherbe* (Paris, 1965), p. 274; hereafter cited in the text as *P*. See also Sollers, pp. 33-35 for a discussion of metaphor.
3. Ian Higgins, "Francis Ponge," in *Sensibility and Creation*, ed. Roger Cardinal (London, 1977), p. 183.
4. Y. Gohin, "Francis Ponge et la poésie contemporaine," (1958), quoted in Sollers, p. 113.

5. See *Méthodes*, p. 270:"Dans tous grands poètes il y a par-ci,par-là, des indications de la sensibilité aux choses, bien sûr, mais c'est toujours noyé dans un flot humain, lyrique, où on vous dit: 'les choses, on y est sensible, mais comme moyen de se parler d'homme à homme.'"

6. Neal Oxenhandler has given considerable attention to this question in "The quest for pure consciousness in Husserl and Mallarmé," in *The quest for imagination in twentieth century aesthetic criticism*, ed. O.B. Hardison (Cleveland, 1971).

7. Sollers, p. 16.

8. Sartre, "L'Homme et les choses," in *Situations I* (Paris, 1947), 259.

9. Beth Archer, *The voice of things*, (New York, 1972) pp. 10-11.

10. Sartre, p. 254.

11. Sollers, p. 20.

12. Sartre, p. 286.

13. Jean-Pierre Richard, *Onze études sur la poésie moderne* (Paris, 1964), pp. 168, 173.

14. In a letter to Godwin, September 1800; quoted in T. Hawkes, *Metaphor* (London, 1972), p. 53.

15. See "Hommage à Francis Ponge," *NRF*, 4, no. 45 (September 1956), 418.

16. Ponge, *Le Savon* (Paris, 1967), p. 127; hereafter cited in the text as *S*.

17. Thibaudeau, p. 80.

18. Werner Wider, *La perception de Ponge* (Zurich, 1974), p. 132.

19. Sartre, p. 274.

20. Ponge, *Pièces* (vol. 3 of *Le Grand Recueil* [Paris, 1961]), p. 156; hereafter cited in the text as *Pi*.

21. Thibaudeau, p. 113.

22. Neal Oxenhandler, "Cocteau, Breton and Ponge," in *About French poetry from Dada to "Tel Quel"*, ed. M.A. Caws (Detroit, 1974), p. 64.

23. Richard, p. 164.

24. Albert Léonard, *La Crise du concept de littérature en France au XXe siècle* (Paris, 1974), p. 104.

25. Oxenhandler, "Cocteau, Breton and Ponge," p. 65.

26. Sollers, p. 58.

27. Higgins, p. 194.

28. Georges-Emmanuel Clancier, *La Poésie et ses environs* (Paris, 1973), p. 243.

29. Higgins, p. 199.

30. Sollers, p. 48.

31. Ibid., p. 25.

32. Ponge, *Lyres* (vol. 1 of *Le Grand Recueil* [Paris, 1961]), p. 150; hereafter cited in the text as *L*.

33. Léonard, p. 130.

34. Thibaudeau, p. 68.

35. Clancier, p. 246.

36. Sollers, pp. 50-51.
37. G. Garampon, "Francis Ponge ou la Résolution humaine"; quoted in Sollers, p. 94.
38. Clancier, p. 243.
39. Sollers, p. 51.
40. Wider, pp. 99-100.
41. Thibaudeau, p. 121.

Chapter Three

1. This phrase has been borrowed from K.K. Ruthven, *The Conceit* (London, 1969).
2. Jean-Luc Lemichez, "Origines inscrites," *Revue des Sciences humaines* (1973), vol. XXXVIII no. 151, 429.
3. Thibaudeau, p. 67.
4. See also "Les olives" (in *Pièces*) for the same importance attached to the circumflex.
5. Higgins, p. 199.
6. Richard, p. 166.
7. Ibid., p. 162.
8. Sartre, pp. 254, 256, 258, 269, 282.
9. Higgins, p. 188.
10. Richard, p. 177.
11. Sartre, p. 286.
12. In "Hommage à Francis Ponge," p. 411.
13. Richard, pp. 168, 173.
14. Sartre, pp. 286-87.
15. Higgins, pp. 193, 200.
16. Ibid., p. 194.
17. Richard, p. 174.
18. Sollers, p. 25.
19. Quoted in Sollers, p. 115.
20. Ibid., p. 128.
21. See *Pour un Malherbe*, p. 248 for comments on rhyme.
22. Higgins, pp. 194-95.
23. *Pour un Malherbe*, pp. 249, 275, 309 all show Ponge's interesting approach to issues of prosody. He proposes one or two highly idiosyncratic technical analyses of particular lines.
24. Wider, p. 35.
25. Oxenhandler, "Cocteau, Breton and Ponge," p. 64.
26. Sartre, p. 248.
27. Ibid., p. 281.
28. Elaine Marks, ed., *French poetry from Baudelaire to the present* (New York, 1962), pp. 33-34.

29. G. Zeltner-Neukomm, "Un poète de natures mortes," in "Hommage à Francis Ponge," p. 424.

30. J. Grenier, "Présentation de Francis Ponge," in "Hommage à Francis Ponge," p. 395.

31. Marks, p. 33.

32. If metaphor does apparently get in the way of an object's self-expression, it is worth recalling Proust's belief, stated in *Le temps retrouvé*, that it discloses the timeless essence of things.

33. Sartre, pp. 292-93.

34. This analysis derives from that offered by T. Hawkes in his *Metaphor*.

35. Oxenhandler, "Ontological criticism in America and France," *Modern Language Review*, 55 (1960), 22-23.

36. Higgins, p. 200.

Chapter Four

1. Lemichez, pp. 414-17.

2. By Cid Corman, *Things* (New York, 1971), pp. 106-8; and by S. Watson Taylor and E. Lucie-Smith, *French poetry today*, pp. 268-75.

3. Richard, p. 180.

Chapter Five

1. A. Robbe-Grillet, speaking of the same neutral attitude, puts it most succinctly: "Or le monde n'est ni signifiant ni absurde. Il *est*, tout simplement." (*Pour un nouveau roman* [Paris, 1963], p.18).

2. Sartre, p. 248.

3. Robbe-Grillet, pp. 63-64.

Selected Bibliography

PRIMARY SOURCES

Much of Ponge's output has appeared as individual texts printed separately, often in expensive and limited editions. A full list of these appears in Jean Thibaudeau, *Ponge* (Paris, 1967), pp. 261-69, and is followed by a good bibliography of secondary material. However, as Thibaudeau's book appeared in 1967, neither of his bibliographies is up-to-date. Marcel Spada, in his 1974 volume on Ponge in the "Poètes d'aujourd'hui" series (no. 220, not to be confused with the earlier no. 95 by Philippe Sollers), brings the bibliography of Ponge's texts more or less up to the present date, but does not include secondary sources. Spada also lists Ponge's works in translation. The list below includes the most important editions of Ponge's works.

Douze petits écrits. Paris: NRF, 1926.
Le Parti pris des choses. Paris: NRF, 1942.
Le Carnet du bois de pins. Lausanne: Mermod, 1947.
Le Peintre à l'étude. Paris: NRF, 1948.
Proêmes. Paris: Gallimard, 1948.
My creative method. Zurich: Atlantis-Verlag, 1949.
La Seine. Lausanne: La Guilde du livre, 1950.
La Rage de l'expression. Lausanne: Mermod, 1952.
Le Grand Recueil. 3 vols. Paris: Gallimard, 1961. The volumes are entitled *Lyres*, *Méthodes*, and *Pièces*. *Méthodes* contains "My creative method."
Pour un Malherbe. Paris: Gallimard, 1965.
Tome premier. Paris: Gallimard, 1965. This is made up of "Douze petits écrits," "Le Parti pris des choses," "Proêmes," "La Rage de l'expression," "Le Peintre à l'étude," and "La Seine."
Le Savon. Paris: Gallimard, 1967.
Nouveau Recueil. Paris: Gallimard, 1967.
Entretiens de Francis Ponge avec Philippe Sollers. Paris: Gallimard/ Editions du Seuil, 1970.
La Fabrique du Pré. Geneva: Skira, 1971.
Comment une figue de paroles et pourquoi. Paris: Flammarion, 1977.
Francis Ponge: Colloque de Cerisy. Paris: 10/18, Union Générale d'Éditions, 1977.
L'Atelier contemporain. Paris: Gallimard, 1977.
L'Écrit Beaubourg. Paris: Centre Georges Pompidou, 1977.

SECONDARY SOURCES

1. Studies and Translations of Ponge

ARCHER, BETH. *The voice of things.* New York: McGraw-Hill, 1972. An introductory chapter followed by a wide-ranging selection of translations from Ponge's work.

BIGONGIARI, PIERO. "Un autre Ponge." *Tel Quel*, 8 (1962), 29-33. A very general introduction.

CAMUS, ALBERT. "Lettre au sujet du 'Parti pris' de Francis Ponge," *La Nouvelle Revue Française*, 4, no 45 (September 1956), 386-92. Reprinted in Camus's *Essais* (Paris: Gallimard, "Bibliothèque de la Pléiade," 1956), 1662-68. Ponge's attitude to the nonhuman world seen in terms of the absurd.

CLANCIER, GEORGES-EMMANUEL. "Francis Ponge ou le poète dans tous ses états." In *La Poésie et ses environs.* Paris: Gallimard, 1973, pp. 238-46. A general presentation.

CORMAN, CID. *Things.* New York: Grossmann, 1971. A selection of Ponge's poems in translation.

DOUTHAT, BLOSSOM MARGARET. "Francis Ponge's Untenable Goat," *Yale French Studies*, 21 (1958), 169-81. A detailed analysis, with translation of "La chèvre."

DUNLOP, LANE. *Ponge: "Soap."* London: Jonathan Cape, 1969. A translation of *Le Savon.*

FOWLIE, WALLACE. "Surrealism: a backward glance," *Poetry*, 95 (1960), 365-72. A paragraph on Ponge, situating him within surrealism.

HIGGINS, IAN. "Francis Ponge." In *Sensibility and Creation: Studies in twentieth-century French poetry*, edited by Roger Cardinal, pp. 183-203. London: Croom Helm, 1977. One of the best short accounts of Ponge; intelligent and stimulating, though sometimes obscure.

HOLLER, DENIS. "L'opinion changée quant à Ponge," *Tel Quel*, 28 (1967), 90-93. General, with useful section on the three-part division of *Le Grand Recueil.*

"Hommage à Francis Ponge." *NRF*, 4, no 45 (September 1956), 385-440. A special number on Ponge, containing eight articles by various critics. Includes Camus's letter and two pieces by Ponge himself.

HOY, PETER. *Ponge: Two prose-poems.* Leicester: Black Knight, 1968. Translations of "Le mollusque" and "Le papillon."

———. *Ponge: "Rain," a prose-poem.* London: Poet & Printer, 1969. A translation of "La pluie".

LEMICHEZ, JEAN-LUC. "Origines inscrites," *Revue des Sciences humaines*, vol. XXXVIII no. 151, (1973), 411-33. A valuable analysis of certain precise aspects of Ponge's use of language.

NADAL, OCTAVE. *Francis Ponge: une oeuvre en cours.* Paris: Doucet, 1960. Detailed chronology of the stages in the composition of a few of Ponge's poems.

OXENHANDLER, NEAL. "Cocteau, Breton and Ponge: the situation of the self." In *About French poetry from Dada to "Tel Quel,"* edited by Mary Ann Caws, pp. 54-68. Detroit: Wayne State University Press, 1974. Some useful, philosophically-biased observations.

PLANK, DAVID. "'Le Grand Recueil': Francis Ponge's optimistic materialism." *Modern Language Quarterly*, 26 (1965), 302-17. General; brings in Robbe-Grillet, Sarraute, and Simon.

PRIGENT, CHRISTIAN. "La 'besogne' des mots chez Francis Ponge." *Littérature*, 29 (February 1978), 90-97. On Ponge's linguistic registers, and their sociopolitical implications.

RICHARD, JEAN-PIERRE. "Francis Ponge." In *Onze études sur la poésie moderne*. Paris: Gallimard Éditions du Seuil, 1964, pp. 161-82. One of the most important studies of Ponge.

ROBBE-GRILLET, ALAIN. *Pour un nouveau roman*. Paris: Éditions de Minuit, Collection "Critique," 1963. A major apologia for the new novel, it contains some important pages on Ponge's relationship to this genre.

SAILLET, MAURICE. "Le proête Ponge." *Mercure de France*, June 1949, pp. 305-13. A virulently dismissive criticism.

SARTRE, JEAN-PAUL. "L'Homme et les choses." In *Situations I*. Paris: Gallimard, 1947, pp. 226-70. One of the first and best appraisals of Ponge. Sartre relates *Le Parti pris des choses* to phenomenology.

SOLLERS, PHILIPPE. *Francis Ponge*. Collection "Poètes d'aujourd'hui," no. 95. Paris: Seghers, 1963. Now superseded by Spada's book, but remains helpful.

SPADA, MARCEL. *Francis Ponge*. Collection "Poètes d'aujourd'hui," no. 220. Paris: Seghers, 1974. Like its predecessor in the series, a useful general introduction, although perhaps less so than Soller's book.

TEMMER, MARK J. "Francis Ponge: a dissenting view of his poetry." *Modern Language Quarterly*, 29 (1968), 207-21. Thoughtful and cautious, it is largely unfavorable in its evaluation of the problems of aesthetics raised by Ponge's poetry.

THIBAUDEAU, JEAN. *Ponge*. Collection "La Bibliothèque Idéale." Paris: Gallimard, 1967. Useful general presentation. Very good bibliography, although not up-to-date.

WALTHER, ELIZABETH. "Caractéristiques sémantiques dans l'oeuvre de Francis Ponge," *Tel Quel*, 31 (1967), 81-84. Examines the notion of semantic beauty in Ponge's aesthetics.

WIDER, WERNER. *La perception de Ponge*. Zurich: Juris Druck & Verlag, 1974. Somewhat given to critical jargon, it has some interesting pages on Ponge and phenomenology.

WILLARD, NANCY. "A poetry of things: Williams, Rilke, Ponge." *Comparative Literature*, 17 (1965), 311-24. A comparative study of these three writers, not really long enough to be other than generalized, although it raises matters of interest.

152

————. *Testimony of the invisible man.* Columbia: University of Missouri Press, 1970. A relatively short chapter on Ponge in a large book covering Williams, Rilke, and Neruda, as well as Ponge.

2. Background Studies

BRAY, RENÉ, ed. *Anthologie de la poésie précieuse.* Paris: Nizet, 1957.

BRETON, ANDRÉ. *Manifeste du surréalisme.* Paris: Kra, 1929.

————. *Flagrant délit.* Paris: Thésée, 1949.

DANTO, ARTHUR. *Sartre.* Modern Masters Series, London: Fontana, 1975.

HAWKES, TERENCE. *Metaphor.* The Critical Idiom Series. London: Methuen, 1972.

JAEGER, HANS. "Heidegger and the work of art." *Journal of Aesthetics and Art Criticism,* 17, no. 1 (1958), 58-71.

LÉONARD, ALBERT. *La Crise du concept de littérature en France au XXe siècle.* Paris: Corti, 1974.

MARKS, ELAINE. ed. *French poetry from Baudelaire to the present.* New York: Dell, 1962.

OXENHANDLER, NEAL. "Ontological criticism in America and France." *Modern Language Review,* 55 (1960), 16-23.

————. "The quest for pure consciousness in Husserl and Mallarmé." In *The quest for imagination in twentieth century aesthetic criticism,* edited by O.B. Hardison. Cleveland: Case Western Reserve University Press, 1971.

RUTHVEN, K. K. *The Conceit.* The Critical Idiom Series. London: Methuen, 1969.

RENARD, JULES. *Histoires naturelles.* Paris: Flammarion, 1896.

STURROCK, JOHN. *The French New Novel.* London: Oxford University Press, 1969.

TAYLOR, SIMON WATSON, and LUCIE-SMITH, EDWARD, eds. *French poetry today.* New York: Schocken Books, 1971.

WARNOCK, MARY. *The philosophy of Sartre.* London: Hutchinson, 1965.

Index